INSIGHTS AND IDEAS

INSIGHTS AND IDEAS

A Beginning Reader
for Students of English
as a Second Language

PATRICIA ACKERT

University of Arizona
Center for English as a Second Language

Harcourt Brace & Company

Orlando   San Diego   New York
Toronto   London   Sydney   Tokyo

NORTH ISLAND COLLEGE

Illustrations by Patricia Phelan Eisenberg.

Library of Congress Cataloging in Publication Data

Ackert, Patricia.
    Insights and ideas.
    Includes index.
    1. English language – Textbooks for foreigners.
2. Readers – 1950–   I. Title.
PE1128.A298   428.6′4   81-6510
ISBN 0-03-058322-5

Requests for permission to make copies of any part of the work should be
mailed to: Permissions Department, Harcourt Brace & Company, 8th Floor,
Orlando, Florida 32887.

    3 4 016 15 14 13

TO THE INSTRUCTOR

This book assumes that the student has a 1,000-word vocabulary. It is designed to teach another 1,000 words plus the reading skills of comprehension; finding the main idea; making inferences; and using context clues, prefixes, and suffixes to learn new words.

An *Instructor's Manual* with answers to all the exercises is available. The Manual also includes a quiz for each lesson, a midterm and a final exam, and a list of new words and irregular verbs in each lesson. The Manual may be obtained through a local Holt representative or by writing to the English Editor, College Department, Holt, Rinehart and Winston, 383 Madison Avenue, New York, NY 10017.

Vocabulary.   Most lessons have ten to fifteen new words that are used several times in the exercises. They also appear several times in later lessons—in the reading selections, the vocabulary review exercises, and the other exercises. Word form exercises increase the number of new vocabulary items to about 1,000.

Vocabulary is one of the most important aspects of language learning for beginning students. The students invariably resort to the tedious memorization of lists of English words with their translation from a bilingual dictionary. I hope they will avoid that with this book.

Some of the new words have a definition or an illustration in the margin the first time they appear. The meanings of others will be clear from the context. Each lesson ends with a context clues exercise that teaches some of the words from the next lesson as well as the skill of using context clues. The students should be encouraged to use the dictionary only as a last resort. The new words should not be taught before the student reads the lesson.

Because the vocabulary is introduced gradually and then used repeatedly in later lessons, the lessons should be done in order. Otherwise the students will be confronted with too many new words at one time.

Structure.   The first few lessons have short, simple sentences. The sentences become longer and more difficult as the lessons progress. All verb tenses except the future perfect are used. Modals are used, and the passive is introduced in Lesson 8. The book also uses all personal pronouns, including the reflexive forms, the past participle as an adjective, gerunds, and such connectors as *although, nevertheless, whether, yet,* and *so.*

EXERCISES

I. Vocabulary. The sentences are taken directly from the reading selection for the first vocabulary practice. All new words are included. The students should refer to the reading for the sentence if they do not know a word. They should not look up the list of words in the dictionary before doing the exercise.

II. Vocabulary. The new words are used again in a different context but with the same meaning. The exercise includes all new words except those that are rarely used, such as *harpoon* and the names of plants in Lesson 13.

III. Vocabulary Review. This exercise reviews words that have not been used in other reading selections or exercises.

IV. Oral Questions. These are comprehension questions. They are specific and easy in the first lessons, but they become more general and harder in later lessons. Those marked with an asterisk (*) are inference questions. There is usually one correct answer, but sometimes there is room for different opinions. The students will probably have trouble with these at first. I suggest that you spend some time having the students find the sentences that support the inference. They quickly learn how to do these questions.

There are no discussion questions on the ideas in the selection because I do not think that discussing ideas teaches reading skills. These oral questions are too hard for most students to answer as written homework.

V. Comprehension. The comprehension questions are either multiple choice or true/false. They include inference questions. There are also a few special exercises, for example, a time line in the lesson on Hawaii, a language chart in Lesson 8, and questions using a graph and tables in a lesson on population growth in third world cities.

VI. Main Idea. Students must select from one to four main ideas in each selection. This exercise is hard for them at first, and it is a good idea to discuss the differences between the main ideas and the supporting details. In a few lessons the students must organize supporting details under the correct main ideas.

Word Study Exercises

Most of the word study exercises are based on other forms of words used in the reading selections. Many of the forms are included in more than one exercise. For example, a word form chart includes *persuade, persuasion, persuasive*. An exercise on the adjective suffix *-ive* also includes *persuasive*. Prefixes and suffixes taught with several words in an exercise are used on different words in reading selections.

Word Forms, Suffixes, and Prefixes.   As explained earlier, these exercises use words from the selections to expand the students' vocabularies. The exercises in the first few lessons teach rules for selecting the correct word forms; for example, the direct object is a noun or pronoun, the subject is a noun or pronoun, an adjective precedes a noun, and so on. As the students do later exercises, it would be helpful to have them give the reason they chose the form for at least a few items in each exercise.

Prepositions.   The first lessons teach the use of a few prepositions. In later lessons the sentences review those uses or are taken directly from the reading selection.

Irregular Verbs.   Five exercises give the forms of the irregular verbs that the students are least likely to know. The *Instructor's Manual* lists all irregular verbs and the lessons where they first appear.

Noun Substitutes.   Four exercises give the students practice in identifying the antecedents of noun substitutes. If the class finds this difficult, you may want to have them identify a few in each lesson until they can do it easily.

Context Clues.   The last exercise helps students learn new words from the context. Most of the words are new vocabulary items from the succeeding lesson, but because many of these are Spanish or French cognates, I have also included words that students are very unlikely to know. The students should learn the skill, not these words. The students may find this exercise difficult at first, but they improve after a few lessons.

ACKNOWLEDGMENTS

I wish to thank Barbara Buchanan, Utah State University; Carolyn Raphael, Queensborough Community College; Penelope Ann Shaw, University of Massachusetts; Amy L. Sonka, Boston University; and Betty Sutton, Ohio State University for reading the manuscript and sharing their ideas with me. Melinda Curry not only typed the manuscript for me but edited as she typed. Julia Braithwaite was always ready to answer my questions as I wrote the lessons. I appreciate their help very much. Susan Katz, my editor, did an outstanding job under unusual circumstances. Shortly after I sent in the manuscript, I left to teach English in China for a year. Ms. Katz helped to ready the manuscript for editorial production even though I was in Beijing and communication was slow. I am very grateful for the extra effort she made.

P.A.

CONTENTS

INSIGHTS AND IDEAS

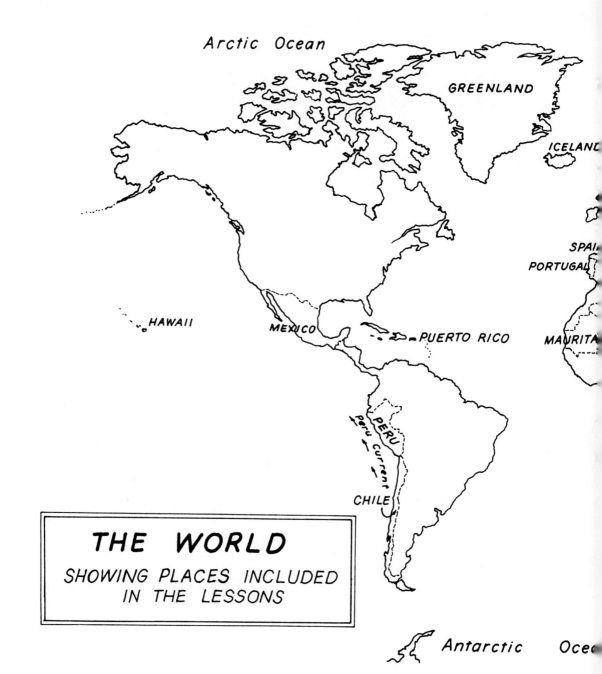

Arctic Ocean

GREENLAND

ICELAND

SPAIN

PORTUGAL

MAURITA

HAWAII

MEXICO

PUERTO RICO

PERU

Peru Current

CHILE

THE WORLD
SHOWING PLACES INCLUDED
IN THE LESSONS

Antarctic Oce

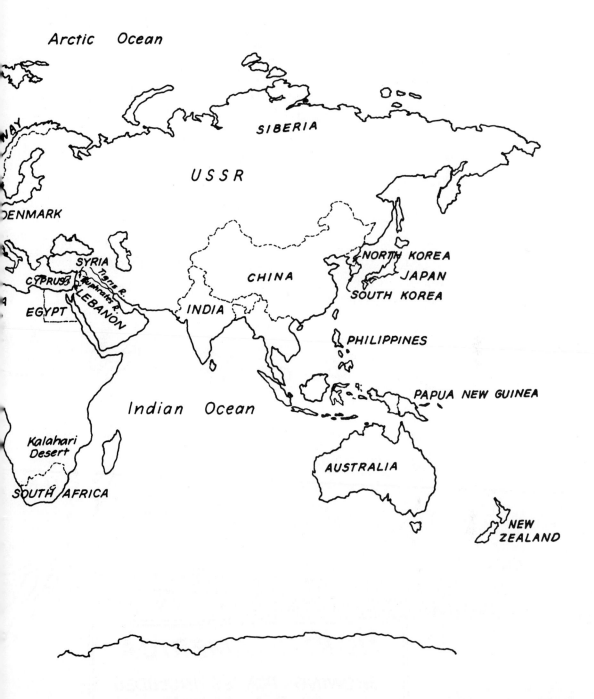

Arctic Ocean

SIBERIA

USSR

NORWAY

DENMARK

SYRIA

CYPRUS

Tigris R.

Euphrates R.

EGYPT

LEBANON

CHINA

INDIA

NORTH KOREA

JAPAN

SOUTH KOREA

PHILIPPINES

PAPUA NEW GUINEA

Indian Ocean

Kalahari
Desert

SOUTH AFRICA

AUSTRALIA

NEW
ZEALAND

1

ALASKA

BRITISH
COLUMBIA

C A

Banf.

Fraser R.

PACIFIC

OCEAN

CALIFORNIA

U N I

San Francisco

Los Angeles

A

NORTH AMERICA
SHOWING PLACES INCLUDED
IN THE LESSONS

TO THE STUDENT

Each lesson in this book has a short reading selection and several exercises.

Some of the questions have an asterisk (*) in front of them. This means that you cannot find the exact answer in the reading. You have to use the information in the selection and the things you know already. Then you have to decide what the right answer is.

The last exercise in each lesson is to help you learn new words. Do not use the dictionary for this exercise. Use the meaning of the complete sentence or paragraph to understand the new word. This is a way to learn the new words for the next lesson.

I hope you enjoy this book. There are many interesting things happening in the world. You can read about some of them in your new language.

Patricia Ackert

FAST-FOOD
RESTAURANTS

Everybody knows that the <u>favorite</u> food in the United   (liked most)
States is the hamburger. It seems impossible, but people
eat 34,000,000,000 (34 billion) hamburgers a year. This
is enough to make a line of hamburgers around the world
four times.

The favorite place to buy a hamburger is a fast-food
restaurant. In these restaurants, people order their food,

wait just a few minutes, and carry it to their tables themselves. They can eat it in the restaurant or take the food
10 out and eat it at home, at work, or in a park. At some
restaurants people can drive up beside a window. They
order the food, and a worker hands it to them through
the window. Then they eat in their car.

Hamburgers are not the only kind of food that fast-
15 food restaurants serve. Some serve fish, chicken, beef
sandwiches, or Mexican food. They also serve fries
(French fried potatoes), shakes (a drink made from milk
and ice cream), soft drinks, and coffee.

Fast-food restaurants are very popular because the
20 service is fast and the food is inexpensive. (Inexpensive
food does not cost very much.) For many people, this
is more important than the quality of the food. These
restaurants are also popular because the food is always
the same. People know that if they eat at a company's
25 restaurant in the north or south of the city, the food will
be the same. If they eat in New York or San Francisco,
it will still be the same.

Fast service and low cost are important in the United
States. One reason is that about 50 percent (50%) of
30 all married women with children work outside the home.
They are too busy and too tired to cook dinner every
night.

Is the food at fast-food restaurants good for you? In
general, it is all right, except that it has too much fat
35 and salt.

One thing is sure. People will continue to eat fast
foods. In fact, now there are fast-food restaurants in
countries all over the world.

hamburger

shake

(how good it is)

fries

(everywhere)

I. VOCABULARY

Choose the best word for each sentence. Use each word only once.

quality	in general	restaurant	all over	percent
billion	favorite	serve	million	still
shakes	service	salt	fries	hamburger

1. Everybody knows that the _____ food in the United States is the hamburger.
2. People eat 34 _____ hamburgers a year.
3. The favorite place to buy a _____ is a fast-food restaurant.
4. Hamburgers are not the only kind of food that fast-food restaurants _____.
5. They also usually serve _____ and _____.
6. Fast-food restaurants are popular because the _____ is fast.
7. For many people, this is more important than the _____ of the food.
8. If they eat in New York or San Francisco, the food will _____ be the same.
9. About 50 _____ of all married women with children work outside the home.
10. _____, fast food is all right.
11. Now there are fast-food restaurants in countries _____ the world.

II. VOCABULARY (new context)

Choose the best word for each sentence. Use each word only once.

in general	billion	service	percent	all over
favorite	million	served	still	quality

1. Ten is ten _____ of one hundred.
2. Which airline gives the best _____?
3. What is your _____ color?
4. You can find people who speak English _____ the world.
5. _____, people study English in high school.
6. Before you buy something, see if the _____ is good.
7. It is June, but it is _____ too cold to go swimming.
8. About one _____ people live in China.
9. Who is usually _____ food first in your country?

III. ORAL QUESTIONS

1. What is the favorite food in the United States?
2. What is the favorite place to buy a hamburger?

3. How do people get their food in a fast-food restaurant?
4. When people buy hamburgers at fast-food restaurants, where do they eat them?
5. What other kinds of food do fast-food restaurants serve?
6. What are fries?
7. What are shakes made from?
8. What are three reasons that fast-food restaurants are popular?
9. Which is least important to many people—speed, quality, or cost?
10. What is one reason that fast service and low cost are important?
11. In general, is fast food good for you?
12. What are two things about fast food that are not very good for you?
13. Are there fast-food restaurants in other countries?

IV. COMPREHENSION

Put a circle around the letter of the best answer.

Questions 6 and 7 have an asterisk (*) in front of them. This means that you cannot find the exact answer in the reading. You have to use the information in the selection and the things you already know. Then you have to decide what the right answer is.

1. People in the United States eat 34 _____ hamburgers a year.
   a. hundred   c. million
   b. thousand   d. billion
2. In a fast-food restaurant _____.
   a. people stand up to eat
   b. a waiter serves people at tables
   c. people carry their food to a table themselves
   d. there are no tables
3. Fast food is _____.
   a. expensive   c. unpopular
   b. inexpensive   d. of high quality
4. About _____ percent of mothers work in the United States.
   a. twenty   c. fifty
   b. forty   d. seventy
5. Fast food has too much _____.
   a. sugar and milk   c. meat and salt
   b. salt and fat   d. beef and fish

*6. People in the United States probably eat too much _____.
   a. fish and chicken   c. beef and salt
   b. fat and salt   d. ice cream and milk
*7. Which answer is NOT true?
   Fast-food restaurants are inexpensive because _____.
   a. the menu changes three times a week
   b. there are no waiters
   c. the food is easy to cook
   d. each restaurant serves only a few different things

V. MAIN IDEA

Choose the two main ideas in the reading. These are the important, general ideas.

_____ 1. Fast-food restaurants are very popular.
_____ 2. People in the United States eat enough hamburgers to make a line around the world four times.
_____ 3. The food in fast-food restaurants is inexpensive, and the service is fast.
_____ 4. Some people eat fast food in parks.
_____ 5. Mothers who work outside the home are often too tired to cook.

WORD STUDY

I. COMPOUND WORDS

It is common to put a verb and another word together to make one word. This word is usually a noun or an adjective. Read these sentences. Then choose the right word for each blank.

1. You can take out food from a fast-food restaurant and eat it at home.
2. If there is any food left over after dinner, save it for tomorrow.

3. When children are grown up, they start drinking coffee.
4. Students often get together on weekends to talk and listen to music.
5. After the people are in a plane, it takes off into the air.

leftovers   takeoff   takeout   grown-ups   get-together

1. Most American _____ drink coffee.
2. After _____ the people on a plane are usually served some food.
3. The students got some _____ food at a fast-food restaurant on their way home from class.
4. People often eat _____ for lunch.
5. Grandparents always enjoy a family _____.

II. PREPOSITIONS

to—shows movement

    She goes to class in the morning.
    John walked to a restaurant at noon.

at—shows location (place) or time

    She usually has dinner at home at six o'clock.

Note: in the morning   at noon
      in the afternoon   at night
      in the evening   at midnight
                         at 7:00, 6:30, 4:23, and so on

Write to, at, or in in the blanks.

1. Students often go to a fast-food restaurant _____ the evening before they go _____ bed.
2. People can eat fast food _____ home or take it _____ a park.
3. People do not eat hamburgers _____ the morning, but they eat them _____ noon and _____ the evening.
4. People carry their own food _____ a table.

5. They eat dinner _____ 6:30 _____ the evening.
6. He usually goes _____ bed _____ 11:00 _____ night.
7. Students eat hamburgers and fries _____ almost any time of the day or night.
8. Fast-food restaurants are popular _____ the United States.
9. They are popular _____ New York and _____ San Francisco.
10. We are going _____ Houston for our vacation.

III. PREFIXES: Negatives un- im- in- dis- non- = not

Write the correct word in the blank.

incomplete	impossible	unsafe	nonsmokers
inexpensive	dishonest	nonstop	unable
disagrees	unpopular		

1. Fast food is _____. It does not cost very much.
2. It seems _____ that people in the United States eat 34 billion hamburgers a year.
3. The student was _____ to come to class because she was sick.
4. There is _____ air service between Los Angeles and Houston. The plane does not stop until it gets to Houston.
5. A person who is unfriendly is probably _____ too.
6. His homework was _____ because he did not have time to finish it.
7. The old bridge is closed because it is _____.
8. I did not buy a car from him because I knew he was _____.
9. _____ sit in the front of a plane. Smokers sit in the back.
10. He _____ with me. He says mothers should not work.

IV. WORD FORMS: Nouns

Every sentence must have a verb.
The subject of a sentence is a noun. (It can also be a pronoun.)

Underline the verb in each sentence.
Write the subject in the blank. Use the noun form of the verb.
Some of the nouns should be plural.

-ment		-er (people)		same	
Verb	**Noun**	**Verb**	**Noun**	**Verb**	**Noun**
govern	government	drive	driver	order	order
agree	agreement	own	owner	drink	drink
		run	runner	cost	cost
		speak	speaker	work	work
		work	worker		

(run)   1. The fastest _____ will win the race.

(drive)   2. A bus _____ will not drive an unsafe bus.

(agree)   3. OPEC decided that oil prices will stay the same for six months. This _____ is very important.

(order)   4. Your _____ is ready. That will be $3.28.

(drink)   5. Soft _____ are very popular all over.

(speak)   6. The _____ spoke for forty minutes.

(govern)   7. The city _____ decided to fix some streets.

(cost)   8. The _____ of fast food is low.

(work)   9. _____ at fast-food restaurants do not make much money.

(work)   10. The _____ on the new bridge is almost complete.

(own)   11. The _____ of the new restaurant on Main Street is Italian.

THE SHOPPING CENTER

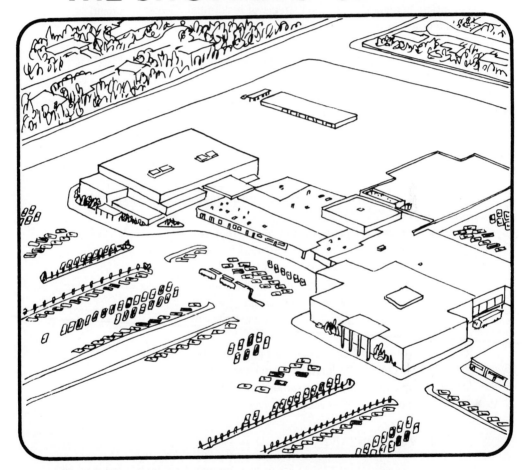

Since 1945 there has been an important change in cities in the United States and Canada—the growth of shopping centers or malls.

Before World War II (1939–1945), cities had depart-

5 ment stores, other smaller stores, and offices. These were in the center of the city, called downtown. Around downtown there were residential areas with houses and apartments.

After World War II, as cities grew larger and larger, it
10 became more and more difficult to drive downtown to go shopping. Store owners decided they could do more business if they left downtown and moved closer to the new residential areas. As a result, today we find large and small shopping centers on the <u>main</u> streets of residential   (most important)
15 areas. Downtown in most cities is not as important as it was before 1945.

A large shopping center or mall has fifty to one hundred stores of all kinds with a large parking lot for cars around it. It is near a residential area, not downtown, and
20 parking in the parking lot is free. There may be two or more department stores that sell everything you can <u>imagine</u>—clothes, gardening equipment, sports equip-   (think of) ment, <u>toys</u>, cameras, records, and books. They also sell   (things children play with) furniture, dishes, towels, and other things for the home.
25 There is often a restaurant that serves complete meals and sandwiches.

Some shopping centers have a supermarket that sells food. There is also a drugstore that sells medicine and hundreds of other things. The other stores usually sell
30 only one kind of thing—books, records, cheese, shoes, clothes for young people, sports and camping equipment, or anything else imaginable. There are usually one or two fast-food restaurants.

Today most stores in shopping centers belong to large
35 companies. These companies have stores in cities all over the country. People can shop in the same store in Toronto or Montreal, in Boston or Chicago, in Denver or Dallas.

I. VOCABULARY

Choose the best word for each sentence. Use each word only once.

imagine	department	mall	supermarket
areas	toys	residential	parking lot
towels	main	dishes	equipment

1. Before World War II, cities had _____ stores downtown.
2. Around downtown there were _____ areas with houses and apartments.
3. Store owners decided to move closer to the new residential _____.
4. Today we find shopping centers on the _____ streets of residential areas.
5. A large shopping center or _____ has fifty to one hundred stores.
6. Parking in the _____ is free.
7. Department stores sell everything you can _____.
8. They sell furniture, _____, and _____ for the house.
9. They also sell gardening _____ and _____.

II. VOCABULARY (new context)

Choose the best word for each sentence. Use each word only once.

lot	toys	serve	dishes
mall	towel	areas	department
residential	main	imagine	equipment

1. Who is going to wash the _____ after dinner?
2. _____ areas are much quieter than business areas.
3. Can you _____ going to a shopping center with a million dollars?
4. Mr. Brown parked his car in the parking _____.
5. A photographer has a lot of _____ for taking pictures.
6. When you go swimming, take a large _____ with you.
7. Dr. Johnson teaches in the English _____ at the university.
8. The children left their _____ all over the living room floor.
9. What is the _____ reason you want to learn English?
10. There are large desert _____ in Asia and Africa.

III. ORAL QUESTIONS

1. What is a change in North American cities since World War II?
2. What is the center of a city called?

3. Why did store owners move their stores to shopping centers?
4. Where do we find shopping centers today?
5. Is downtown as important today as it was before 1945?
6. What is around the stores in a shopping center?
7. What do department stores sell?
8. Can you eat in a department store?
9. What does a drugstore sell?
10. What do other stores in malls sell?
11. Are there fast-food restaurants in malls?
12. Who do most stores in malls belong to?

IV. COMPREHENSION: True/False

Write *T* if the sentence is completely true. Write *F* if it is completely or partly false.

_____ 1. A mall is a shopping center.
_____ 2. Before World War II there were shopping centers around downtown.
_____ 3. It is often difficult to drive downtown in big cities.
_____ 4. The downtown area is usually a residential area.
_____ 5. Shopping centers are on main streets in residential areas.
_____ *6. People like shopping centers because they can buy everything in one place, and parking is free.
_____ *7. A shopping center is a good place to buy birthday presents.
_____ *8. It is difficult for a person to start a small business in a mall.

V. MAIN IDEA

Choose the three main ideas.

_____ 1. Shopping centers are on main streets in residential areas.
_____ 2. Shopping centers are an important change in cities.
_____ 3. Shopping centers have a drugstore that sells medicine.
_____ 4. Shopping centers have large parking lots.
_____ 5. Shopping centers have many kinds of stores.

WORD STUDY

I. SUFFIXES: -th Nouns

Read the sentences. Then choose the best word for each blank.

Some cities grow quickly. Their growth is fast.
That street is five kilometers long. The length of that street is five kilometers.
The street is fifteen meters wide. Its width is fifteen meters.
The lake is thirty meters deep. Its depth is thirty meters.
He is very strong. He has a lot of strength in his arms.
BUT:
How high is that building? What is its height?
How much do you weigh? What is your weight?

strength   growth   length   width   depth   height   weight

1. Some trees grow to a _____ of 65 meters.
2. The _____ of the Golden Gate Bridge in San Francisco is about 1,400 meters.
3. What is the _____ of the Pacific Ocean at its deepest point?
4. A weight lifter has great _____ in his arms.
5. When children do not have enough to eat, their _____ is slow.
6. What is the _____ of your garage? Can you park two cars in it?
7. David is much thinner now. He has lost a lot of _____.

II. PREPOSITIONS

on—over and touching something
   touching something

   The book is on the desk.
   There is a picture on the wall.
   Note: on Monday (days)
          on January 10 (dates)
          on television
          on the radio

in—inside something
     within limits of a space or time

    The cat is in the house.
    They have their vacation in April. (months)
    People like to go swimming in summer. (seasons)
    He was born in 1962. (years)
    I'll meet you in ten minutes.

Write *in, on, at,* or *to* in the blanks.

1. Classes start _____ Monday.
2. They will finish _____ May.
3. I saw a program about shopping centers _____ television.
4. Mr. and Mrs. Johnson are going _____ the mall this afternoon.
5. Shopping centers are _____ residential areas.
6. There are several kinds of stores _____ shopping centers.
7. There is a vacation _____ two weeks.
8. Let's go _____ the new mall.
9. The dishes are _____ the table, and the clothes are _____ the closet.
10. Large companies have stores _____ malls all over the country.
11. I'll meet you _____ the Student Center _____ noon.
12. Shopping centers are usually open _____ Sundays.
13. People drive _____ malls to go shopping.
14. Those new stores opened _____ September 1.
15. Did you buy your furniture _____ a department store?

III. CONTEXT CLUES

You can often understand the meaning of a new word from the other words in a sentence.
For example:
In paragraph 2: "Around downtown there were residential areas with houses and apartments." What are residential areas?
In paragraph 4: "A large shopping center or mall has fifty to one hundred stores of all kinds." What is a mall?
Read the following sentences. Then circle the letter of the best meaning for the underlined word. Don't use the dictionary.

1. Almost every country in Africa was a <u>colony</u> of a European country until 1951.
   a. a large farm that grows coffee or bananas
   b. a place or country that belongs to another country
   c. part of a business
   d. a residential and farming area
2. In the United States, when you buy something, you usually pay a city and state <u>tax</u> on it.
   a. money that goes to the government
   b. money for good service
   c. money for the store owner
   d. money for the bank
3. <u>Codfish</u> is a popular food in Portugal.
   a. a kind of meat
   b. a kind of fish
   c. a kind of vegetable
   d. a kind of fruit
4. Ferdinand Magellan was the first <u>explorer</u> to go around the world.
   a. a person who looks for new places and information about them
   b. a person who looks for new business
   c. a place that is difficult to find
   d. something that an airplane carries
5. The growth of the United States was very fast during the <u>century</u> from 1880 to 1980.
   a. 1,000 years
   b. 10 years
   c. 50 years
   d. 100 years
6. The secretary ordered books, pens, paper, and other <u>supplies</u> for the school.
   a. things they needed
   b. things to write with
   c. things that are inexpensive
   d. things that are in a shopping center
7. There are television and car <u>factories</u> in Japan and clothes <u>factories</u> in Korea.
   a. buildings where they sell cars
   b. buildings where they serve food
   c. buildings where they make something
   d. buildings where they watch television

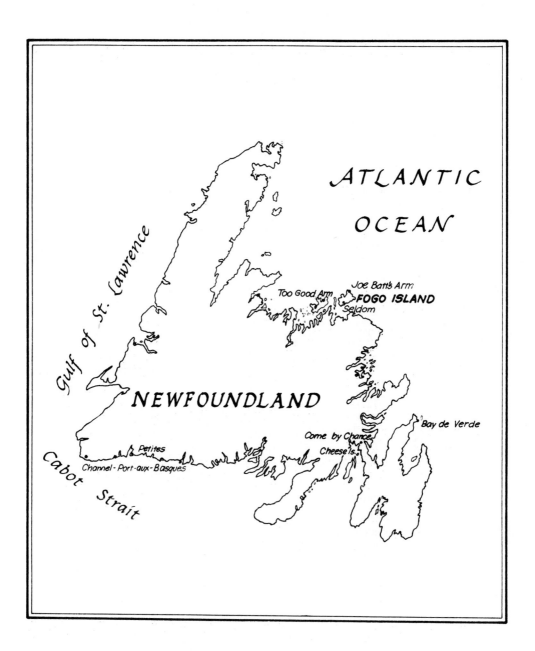

NEWFOUNDLAND[1]

John Cabot's ship

One of the first things you notice when you look at a map of Newfoundland Island is the strange place-names. You see Cheese Island, Bay de Verde, Port-aux-Basques, and Joe Batt's Arm. Then you notice Seldom, Too Good 5 Arm, Petites, Fogo Island, and Come by Chance. Why does an island in eastern Canada have names in four languages.?

[1] Pronunciation: new-fund-lánd or néw-fund-lund.

John Cabot, an English explorer, visited Newfoundland in 1497. <u>However</u>, fishing boats were visiting there for (but)
10 many years before that. There is a very rich fishing area near the island; and French, Portuguese, Basque, and English fishermen came there to catch codfish and other kinds of fish. They dried the fish and took it back to sell in their countries. Over the <u>centuries</u> they visited many (100 years)
15 places on the island and named them.

In 1583 an English ship was on the way to North America to start a colony. The people needed food and other supplies to start a new village. The best place to get them was from the fishing boats. Humphrey Gilbert,
20 the captain of the ship, made Newfoundland an English colony. He said it belonged to England, and the fishing boats had to pay taxes to the English government. He made them give him supplies as their taxes.

England was able to earn a lot of money by selling
25 codfish to other countries. The area was also an excellent place to teach young seamen their new jobs.

However, England did not want people to live there, so for many years there were only a few hundred people living on the island. Most of them lived in small fish-
30 ing villages with no roads. Everyone traveled by boat. Newfoundland did not become part of Canada until 1949.

Even today most of the 500,000 people live in about 1,300 very small coastal villages. Because of this, most people are very independent. They usually do things for
35 themselves, and it is sometimes difficult for them to work together. Sometimes they are afraid of new ideas. For many years they spent the long, cold winter evenings sitting by the fire and telling stories. Now they watch television.
40 Today some people still fish. However, more people work in the modern paper industry. They cut down trees and work in the large factories that make paper. The factories sell the paper to other countries.

Newfoundland is one of the poorest areas of Canada.
45 The people there want to have a better life, but they do not want to change the old ways too much.

I. VOCABULARY

factories	colony	island	industry
explorer	taxes	centuries	supplies
however	in general	earn	independent

1. One of the first things you notice when you look at a map of Newfoundland _____ is the strange place-names.
2. John Cabot, an English _____, visited Newfoundland in 1497.
3. _____, fishing boats were visiting there for many years before that.
4. Over the _____ fishermen visited many places on the island.
5. In 1583, an English ship was on the way to North America to start a _____.
6. It needed food and other _____ to start a new village.
7. The fishing boats had to pay _____ to the English government.
8. England was able to _____ a lot of money by selling codfish.
9. Most people in Newfoundland are very _____.
10. Today people work in the modern paper _____.
11. They cut down trees and work in the large _____ that make paper.

II. VOCABULARY (new context)

colony	supplies	industry	islands
independent	however	century	taxes
factories	imaginable	explorer	in general
earn			

1. There are several car _____ in Detroit.
2. Christopher Columbus was an early _____ who visited the New World.
3. You can buy _____ for a camping trip at a mall.
4. Most African colonies became _____ during the last thirty years.
5. Nobody likes to pay _____.
6. A _____ ago, there were no cars or planes.

7. _____, there were trains.
8. There are two small islands near Newfoundland that are still a French _____. They are not part of Canada.
9. The owner of a factory can _____ a lot of money.
10. Detroit is an important center of the automobile _____.
11. Japan is a group of _____.

III. ORAL QUESTIONS

1. What do you notice when you look at a map of Newfoundland Island?
2. Who was John Cabot?
3. Was Cabot the first European to visit Newfoundland? Explain.
4. What did the fishermen do with the codfish?
5. Why was Humphrey Gilbert going to North America?
6. What did he need?
7. How did he get these supplies?
8. Why was Newfoundland a good colony for England?
9. Where did the people live on the island?
10. Where do most of the people live today?
11. Describe the people of Newfoundland.
12. What kind of work do people do today?
13. Where do the factories sell the paper?
14. What do Newfoundlanders want for the future?

IV. COMPREHENSION

1. Newfoundland has unusual names because _____.
   a. John Cabot visited there
   b. men from several countries fished there
   c. it is in eastern Canada
   d. England sold codfish to different countries
2. John Cabot was an English _____.
   a. explorer   c. colony
   b. fisherman   d. businessman
3. The fishermen _____.
   a. sold their fish to England
   b. bought their fish from England

c. sold their fish in Newfoundland

d. took their fish home with them

4. The fishermen named places on the island _____.

    a. over the centuries

    b. so they could start a colony

    c. for their captains

    d. so they could pay taxes

5. Captain Gilbert was going to _____.

    a. catch fish

    b. name places on the island

    c. start a colony

    d. sell supplies to the fishing boats

6. Today most Newfoundlanders live _____.

    a. in factories

    b. in villages on the coast

    c. in colonies

    d. on their boats in rich fishing areas

7. Today many people work _____.

    a. making paper   c. building ships

    b. selling paper   d. selling supplies

*8. Which one is probably NOT true?

    a. TV has changed the daily life in Newfoundland.

    b. Most Newfoundlanders welcome new ideas.

    c. Most Newfoundlanders live a simple life.

    d. Newfoundlanders do things for themselves.

V. MAIN IDEA

Choose the four main ideas.

_____ 1. Fishing boats have fished near Newfoundland for several centuries.

_____ 2. Newfoundlanders watch TV.

_____ 3. There is a place named Too Good Arm.

_____ 4. Newfoundland became an English colony in 1583 and part of Canada in 1949.

_____ 5. The number of people there grew very slowly.

_____ 6. Fishing boats dried codfish.

_____ 7. Today Newfoundlanders fish and work in the paper industry.

WORD STUDY

I. COMPOUND WORDS

Sometimes you can make a new word by putting two words together. The meaning of the compound word is related to the two words.

Choose the best compound word for each blank.

seamen	horseback	someone	notebook
fireplace	birthday	underline	bedroom
stoplight			

1. You sit on the back of a horse to ride _____.
2. In class, you write notes about what the teacher says in your _____.
3. A place to build a fire in the house is a _____.
4. _____ wants to talk to you on the telephone. I don't know who it is.
5. Cars must stop when the _____ is red.
6. Mr. Brown's daughter had her first _____ one year after her birth. She was one year old.
7. You sleep in a bed in the _____.
8. Put a line under the verb. _____ the verb.

II. SUFFIXES: -al, -able, -ful (full of, having)

An adjective describes a noun or a pronoun.
An adjective is usually before a noun or after the verb <u>be</u>.

Switzerland is a <u>beautiful</u> country.
Switzerland is <u>beautiful</u>.

Write the adjective form of each word. Then write the correct adjective in each blank. Underline the noun or pronoun it describes.
Spelling: Change *y* to *i* before -al and -ful.

Noun	-al Adjective	Verb	-able Adjective	Noun	-ful Adjective
coast	_____	notice	_____	beauty	_____
season	_____	agree	_____	help	_____
industry	_____	enjoy	_____	wonder	_____
nation	_____				

(coast)   1. Most people in Newfoundland live in _____ villages.

(notice)   2. The strange names in Newfoundland are _____ on a map.

(help)   3. Workers in shopping centers are usually _____.

(agree)   4. Are you _____ to this plan?

(industry)   5. Newfoundland is not an _____ center of Canada.

(nation)   6. He plays on the Brazilian _____ soccer team.

(beauty)   7. The Andes Mountains are a _____ sight from a plane.

(season)   8. Skiing is a _____ sport. People ski in winter.

(enjoy)   9. They had an _____ evening at their friends' apartment.

(wonder)   10. London is a _____ city to visit.

III. CONTEXT CLUES

Choose the answer that is closest in meaning to the underlined word. Do not use the dictionary.

1. Today in Saudi Arabia some men wear European clothes, but most people wear traditional clothes.
   a. something from the United States
   b. something to wear in hot weather
   c. something to wear in cold weather
   d. something people have used or worn for many years

2. What is your old car worth if you sell it?
   a. What color is it?
   b. How much is it?
   c. How old is it?
   d. Where did you buy it?

3. <u>Human</u> <u>beings</u> can talk. Animals cannot.
   a. plants
   b. people
   c. cats
   d. children
4. There were several important <u>events</u> the first week of classes—a party, a trip, a meeting, and a long test.
   a. a good time
   b. something that is sad
   c. something that is expensive
   d. something that happens
5. In Canada it is <u>ordinary</u> for children to play ice hockey. This is not <u>ordinary</u> in Mexico.
   a. difficult
   b. strong
   c. independent
   d. usual
6. <u>Pitch</u> the ball to me.
   a. Give
   b. Sell
   c. Throw
   d. Take

COUNTRY MUSIC

Johnny Cash and June Carter Cash

Artist Consultants Productions, Inc., Los Angeles

City people usually think they are a lot smarter than
country people. They often laugh at simple country ways.
But people do not laugh at country music. It is one of the
most popular kinds of music in the United States today.

5   Perhaps it is so popular because it is about simple but
strong human feelings and events—love, sadness, good

times, and bad times. It tells real-life stories and sounds the way people really talk. As life becomes more and more <u>complicated</u>, it is good to hear music about <u>ordinary</u>   (not simple) (usual, regular)
10 people.

Country, sometimes called country-western, comes from two kinds of music. One is the traditional music of the people in the Appalachian Mountains in the eastern United States. The other is traditional cowboy music from
15 the West. The singers usually play guitars, and in the 1920s they started using electric guitars.

At first city people said country music was low class. It was popular mostly in the South. But during World War II, thousands of Southerners went to the Northeast and
20 Midwest to work in the factories. They took their music with them. Soldiers from the rest of the country went to army camps in the South. They learned to like country music. Slowly it became popular all over the country.

In 1925 the radio program called "Grand Ole Opry"
25 (Grand or Wonderful Old Opera) started broadcasting country music from Nashville, Tennessee. Today it broadcasts from the largest television <u>studio</u> in the world, and   (place to make TV and radio programs)
Nashville is the mecca of country music. Musicians make records in almost sixty recording studios that are open
30 twenty-four hours a day, and they sell $400 million (four hundred million dollars) worth of records every year. There are hotels, an entertainment park, stores that sell cowboy clothes, a Country Music Hall of <u>Fame</u>, and tours   (noun for famous)
past the homes of the big stars. Most of these singers were
35 very poor when they were children, but now they live in large, expensive homes. Millions of people have visited Nashville and listened to music there.

Today country music is popular everywhere in the United States and Canada—in small towns and in New
40 York City, among black and white, and among educated and uneducated people. About 1,200 radio stations broadcast country music twenty-four hours a day. English stars sing it in British English, and people in other countries sing it in their languages. The music that started with
45 cowboys and poor Southerners is now popular all over the world.

I. VOCABULARY

uneducated	traditional	ordinary	simple
so	complicated	events	army
smarter	human	worth	program
studio	entertainment	fame	

1. City people usually think they are _____ than country people.
2. They often laugh at _____ country ways.
3. Perhaps country music is _____ popular because it is about strong feelings.
4. It is about simple but strong _____ feelings and _____.
5. As life becomes more and more _____, it is good to hear music about _____ people.
6. Country music comes from the _____ music of the Appalachian Mountains and from cowboy music.
7. Soldiers went to _____ camps in the South.
8. In 1925 the radio _____ called "Grand Ole Opry" started broadcasting.
9. Today it broadcasts from the largest TV _____ in the world.
10. Studios in Nashville sell $400 million _____ of records every year.
11. In Nashville there is a Country Music Hall of _____.

II. VOCABULARY (new context)

ordinary	traditional	so	still
program	event	fame	complicated
worth	army	human	smart
simple			

1. The kimono is the _____ dress in Japan.
2. In many countries, men go into the _____ when they are eighteen.
3. The first _____ on the sports program was a volleyball game.
4. Today it is not necessary to do _____ math problems in your head.

5. Food that is expensive and difficult to find in one country may be inexpensive and _____ in another country.
6. How much is that house _____?
7. He was a rich and famous actor, but his _____ did not bring him happiness.
8. He is _____ strong that he can lift 100 kilos.
9. This is a _____ math problem: 2 + 2 = .
10. Carmen is a _____ student.

III. VOCABULARY REVIEW: Opposites

Match the words that mean the opposite. Write the word from Column B next to the word in Column A that is the opposite.

A	**B**
1. educated	a. rider
2. grown-up	b. dependent
3. incomplete	c. listener
4. driver	d. finished
5. business	e. uneducated
6. independent	f. owner
7. length	g. width
8. agreement	h. child
9. speaker	i. residential
10. strong	j. weak
	k. worth
	l. disagreement

IV. ORAL QUESTIONS

1. What do city people usually think about country people?
2. Why is country music possibly so popular?
3. How does it sound?
4. Where does country music come from?
5. Why did many Southerners go to the Northeast and the Midwest during World War II?

6. Why did other people go to the South?
7. What city is the mecca of country music?
8. What can tourists visit in Nashville?
9. What kind of life did most of the big stars have when they were children?
10. Who likes country music today?

V. COMPREHENSION

1. Country music is about _____.
   - a. different countries
   - b. human feelings and events
   - c. Nashville, Tennessee
   - d. World War II
2. Country music comes from _____.
   - a. the Appalachian Mountains and the West
   - b. the Northeast and Midwest
   - c. the South and Northeast
   - d. factories and army camps
3. At first country music was popular mostly in the _____.
   - a. Northeast and West
   - b. South and Northeast
   - c. factories and army camps
   - d. South
4. Thousands of Southerners went to work in _____.
   - a. Nashville
   - b. the Appalachian Mountains
   - c. factories
   - d. the West
5. Nashville probably does NOT have _____.
   - a. a Baseball Hall of Fame
   - b. a Country Music Hall of Fame
   - c. TV and recording studios
   - d. large, beautiful homes
6. Most country singers _____.
   - a. were born in Nashville
   - b. were poor when they were children
   - c. worked in factories when they were younger
   - d. came to Nashville to live in an army camp
*7. If you want to be a country singer, _____.
   - a. go to Nashville
   - b. become a cowboy
   - c. get a good education
   - d. study music at a university

*8. When countries become more modern, _____.
   a. people move north
   b. radios broadcast country music in English
   c. life becomes more complicated
   d. people sing about their problems

VI. MAIN IDEA

Choose the three main ideas.

_____ 1. City people are smarter than country people.
_____ 2. Country music comes from the Appalachian Mountains and from cowboy music.
_____ 3. It became popular all over the United States and then all over the world.
_____ 4. Modern life is complicated.
_____ 5. Today country music is a business worth millions of dollars.
_____ 6. British singers sing country music.

WORD STUDY

I. PREPOSITIONS: of

belonging to things

   the back of the room
   the arm of the chair
              BUT
   John's arm (person)

with numbers

   one of the students
   thousands of Southerners

with definite and indefinite amounts

a lot <u>of</u> hamburgers
part <u>of</u> the house
half <u>of</u> the students
some <u>of</u> the country musicians

shows a relationship between two nouns

the name <u>of</u> the city
a kind <u>of</u> store
an example <u>of</u> country music

Write *of, at, in, on,* or *to* in the blanks.

1. What kind _____ vegetables do you like?
2. Six _____ the students _____ the class are from the Middle East.
3. You can hear hundreds _____ country songs _____ radio stations.
4. Country music is one example _____ popular music.
5. There will be a country music program _____ February 15.
6. Millions _____ people go _____ Nashville.
7. Radio stations play country music _____ noon, _____ midnight, _____ the morning, and _____ the afternoon.
8. What is the name _____ that song?
9. The walls _____ the room are white.
10. Europeans went _____ Newfoundland to fish.
11. The arm _____ the chair is broken.
12. A lot _____ people in the United States eat in fast-food restaurants.
13. Half _____ the mothers in the United States work outside the home.
14. Some _____ them work _____ factories.

II. CONTEXT CLUES

1. Beginning English classes are <u>limited to twenty people</u> because it is difficult to learn a language in a big class.
   a. taught to twenty people   c. kept larger than twenty people
   b. have twenty people or less   d. introduced to twenty people
2. Before the nineteenth century, Japan had very few visitors from other

countries. The society was very traditional and did not change much. Today Japanese visit other countries and are very interested in learning new things. Foreigners visit Japan and learn from the Japanese. Japanese society is modern but with many traditional ideas.

   a. everything in the life of a group of people or country
   b. businessmen and tourists who travel all over the world
   c. one hundred years
   d. factories where people make TVs and cars

3. Brazil produces coffee, Japan produces cars, and Saudi Arabia produces oil.
   a. grows, makes, or takes out of the ground
   b. buys and sells
   c. drinks, drives, and uses in cars
   d. uses inside the country

4. Mr. Brown had his eightieth birthday last week. All his children, grand-children, cousins, and other relatives came to his party.
   a. uncles and aunts   c. friends
   b. members of the larger family   d. parents

5. Mr. and Mrs. Taylor live in San Francisco. Their daughter is a student in Los Angeles. Their son works in Houston, Texas. The family is separated.
   a. busy   c. not together
   b. small   d. not happy

6. You must have at least sixty correct answers to pass this test. If you have fifty-nine, you do not pass. If you have sixty or more, you pass.
   a. not less than   c. more than
   b. the same as   d. half of

7. Social scientists say the American family is changing fast.
   a. people who study chemistry
   b. people who study engineering
   c. people who study art
   d. people who study society

THE FAMILY

The family in the Western world has changed greatly during the last two centuries. Social scientists say this is one of the important changes from a traditional society to a modern society.

5   Before the nineteenth century, families usually arranged marriages for their children. Young people did not
decide whom they wanted to marry. After they got married, they usually had a lot of children. This family was an
important part of the larger family of aunts, uncles, cou-
10 sins, grandparents, and other relatives.

By the nineteenth century, most young people could
choose whom they wanted to marry. Marriage joined two
people and not two families. The reason two people got
married was because they loved each other. It was not
15 just because the families wanted them to marry.

At the same time, parents began to realize that they
had to take very good care of their children. They had to
take care of their health and try to give them an education. Before this, most people did not go to school. But
20 now education was necessary for a good life.

The parents decided they should have fewer children
so they could give each one a good life. They thought it
was important for the mother to spend as much time as
possible with her children. Before, the family all worked
25 together at home. After 1800 more fathers worked outside the home for money. Mothers stayed home and had
greater control of the home and children. Most homes
did not <u>produce</u> anything. Home was a safe, warm place   (make)
for the father after work and for the mother and small
30 children all day. The other relatives were still important,
but they were <u>separated</u> more than before.   (not together)

Family life is changing even faster in the United States
today. There is almost one <u>divorce</u> for every two mar-   (end of a marriage)
riages. Over 10 percent of families have a mother and
35 children but no father. At least half of all children will
live part of the time with only one parent. Fifty percent of
all mothers work outside the home.

In Canada people are getting divorced and <u>remarried</u>   (married again)
more often. They are having fewer children. This is
40 having a powerful effect on a country where change has
usually been slow.

Some social scientists think that soon there will be no
family life in the United States as we know it today. They
do not know how people will live. Others think society
45 needs families, and we will always have them.

I. VOCABULARY

society	greatly	at least	remarried
divorce	each other	social	produce
relatives	arranged	so	separated
traditional	century	control	realize

1. _____ scientists say the change in family life is very important.
2. It is an important change from a traditional _____ to a modern society.
3. Before the nineteenth century, families usually _____ marriages.
4. By the nineteenth century, the reason two people got married was because they loved _____.
5. Parents began to _____ that they had to take very good care of their children.
6. The parents decided they should have fewer children _____ they could give each one a good life.
7. Mothers stayed home and had greater _____ of the home and children.
8. Most homes did not _____ anything.
9. The other _____ were still important.
10. They were more _____ than before.
11. Today there is almost one _____ for every two marriages in the United States.
12. _____ half of all children will live with only one parent.
13. In Canada people are getting divorced and _____ more often.

II. VOCABULARY (new context)

each other	produce	arranged	at least
relatives	divorce	realize	societies
so	social	control	separated

1. You must read _____ five pages a day to finish the book this year.

2. Several of Keiko's _____ came to the airport when she left for Canada.
3. Mexico and Venezuela _____ oil.
4. I didn't _____ what time it was, and I was late for work.
5. The Millers were not happy with their apartment, so they _____ the furniture in a different way.
6. Japanese and Egyptian _____ are very different.
7. The Peruvian and French students in the class have to speak English to _____.
8. After fifteen years of marriage, the Browns decided to get a _____.
9. In some countries girls and boys are _____ in school. There is a girls' school and a boys' school.
10. The driver lost _____ of his car and hit a tree.

III. VOCABULARY REVIEW

Underline one word that should not be with the other three.

Example: red, <u>book</u>, green, yellow

1. difficult, easy, hard, complicated
2. billion, million, thousand, quality
3. sandwich, shake, hamburger, fries
4. driver, inexpensive, nonsmokers, disagree
5. fireplace, notebook, birthday, explorer
6. pen, towel, dish, bed
7. length, growth, width, depth

IV. ORAL QUESTIONS

1. What has happened to the Western family during the last two centuries?
2. What do social scientists say about this?
3. Who arranged marriages before the nineteenth century?
4. Were families usually large or small?
5. After 1800 why did two people usually get married?
6. What did parents have to do for their children?
7. Why did parents decide to have fewer children?
8. Before 1800 who worked in the family?

9. After 1800 what did mothers do?
10. How did the family feel about their other relatives?
11. How is family life in the United States changing today?
12. Why do changes have a powerful effect in Canada?
13. What do some social scientists think?
14. What do others think?

V. COMPREHENSION

1. The family in the Western world _____ during the last two centuries.
   a. has not changed
   b. has changed a little
   c. has grown
   d. has changed a lot
2. Before the nineteenth century _____.
   a. people got married because they loved each other
   b. families usually arranged marriages
   c. people could choose whom they wanted to marry
   d. young people decided whom they would marry
3. During the 1800s _____.
   a. marriage joined two families
   b. marriage joined two people
   c. parents chose wives for their sons
   d. families arranged marriages
4. Education became necessary _____.
   a. for a good marriage
   b. for good health
   c. for a good life
   d. for a big family
5. All the relatives in the larger family _____ after 1800.
   a. were not important to each other
   b. tried to find good husbands for the daughters
   c. controlled all the children
   d. were still important, but separated more
6. Today family life in Canada and the United States is _____.
   a. changing even faster
   b. still changing, but not as much
   c. not changing at all
   d. changing a little
*7. Which one is probably NOT true?
   a. Life is more complicated in a family with no father.

b. Life is more difficult for children of divorced parents.

c. It is difficult to live in a society that is changing fast.

d. Americans have small families because they do not like children very much.

*8. Social scientists do NOT study _____.

a. family life

b. how a plant can produce more food

c. the differences between life in the city and the country

d. marriage in different countries

VI. MAIN IDEA

Choose the three main differences between families today and families before the nineteenth century.

_____ 1. family size

_____ 2. choosing a wife or husband

_____ 3. a comfortable house

_____ 4. clothes to get married in

_____ 5. the number of divorces

WORD STUDY

I. PREFIXES: re = to do something again

Example: Read the story. Then reread it. (Read it again.)

Add re- to each word. Then put the correct word in each sentence.

order   build   married   tell   arranged   do

1. The Browns did not like the living room in their new apartment, so they _____ the furniture.

2. After his divorce, he _____. He has a new wife now.
3. Children love to hear their grandparents tell and _____ stories.
4. We had to _____ dinner because the waiter forgot our order the first time.
5. The family's house burned down, but they are going to _____ in the same place.
6. Paul had a mistake at the beginning of a long math problem, so he had to _____ the whole thing.

II. WORD FORMS: Nouns

The direct object of a verb is usually a noun. It can also be a pronoun.
The direct object receives the action of the verb.
It answers the question, "What?"

direct object

Example: Families usually arranged marriages.
What did families arrange? Marriages.

Underline the verb. Write a noun for the direct object. Some of the nouns are plural.

-ity		same		different	
Adjective	**Noun**	**Verb**	**Noun**	**Verb**	**Noun**
electric	electricity	change	change	marry	marriage
able	ability	control	control	choose	choice
national	nationality	divorce	divorce		
necessary	necessity				
possible	possibility				

(electric) 1. The electric company turned on the _____ for us.

(change) 2. There has been a great _____ in family life.

(national) 3. She wrote her _____ and language on the paper.

(marry) 4. Parents used to arrange _____.

(control) 5. Mothers had more _____ of the home and children.

(necessary)   6. It is necessary to come to class on time. The teacher explained this _____ to the students.

(divorce)   7. Mr. and Mrs. Smith got a _____.

(able)   8. Some people can learn another language quickly. This
_____ is very useful.

(choose)   9. Mike doesn't know what kind of car to buy. It is hard to
make a _____.

(possible)   10. Ali doesn't know where to go on his vacation. He has
three _____.

III. PREPOSITIONS

by = near

The table is <u>by</u> the chair.

by = along, through, over

They entered the building <u>by</u> the front door.

by = not later than (time)

Please be here <u>by</u> 7:00 P.M. (at 7:00 or before 7:00 but not later
than 7:00)

Put *by, at, in, of, on,* or *to* in the blanks.

1. The teacher's desk is _____ the door.
2. Her books are _____ the desk ready to use.
3. Married people in the United States used to have a lot _____
   children.
4. This family was an important part _____ the larger family.
5. You should be _____ the airport _____ 4:00 to go on the 4:30
   plane. Don't come later than 4:00.
6. Parents had to take care _____ their children.
7. Your seat for the program is _____ the door.
8. Let's drive _____ the new shopping center on our way home. We
   don't have time to stop, but let's look at it as we drive _____.
9. The vacation starts _____ noon _____ Wednesday and ends
   _____ Sunday.
10. The mother had greater control _____ the home and children.

11. José walks _____ the Student Center on his way _____ class _____ the morning.
12. You have to go _____ the restaurant _____ 6:30 to get a table. If you go later, you will have to wait.
13. Family life is changing fast _____ the United States today.
14. Over 10 percent _____ families have no father.
15. Who do you sit _____ in writing class?

IV. CONTEXT CLUES

1. For centuries people have killed elephants in Africa. They want the beautiful white ivory to make jewelry and other things.
   a. skin
   b. something that grows out of an elephant's face
   c. large ears
   d. a long nose that an elephant uses to eat with
2. Mike wants to improve his English so he practices as much as he can.
   a. study   c. write
   b. test   d. make better
3. An art museum has a lot of pictures on the walls. A science museum shows different machines. A history museum has things about the history of a city or an area.
   a. a building where you can see interesting things
   b. a building where people make different things
   c. an event that was important in history
   d. a place where a social scientist lives

4. Some artists make things out of wood. They use a knife to carve them.
   a. write   c. cut
   b. paint   d. sing
5. If you do not know the answer to a question, just guess. Write a, b, c, or d. Choose one letter and write it.
   a. Answer something when you do not know the right answer.
   b. Answer after you look in the dictionary.
   c. Answer after you study the lesson again.
   d. Don't answer the question.
6. People must drink water to live. Water is essential for life.
   a. simple   c. easy
   b. human   d. necessary

ESKIMO ART

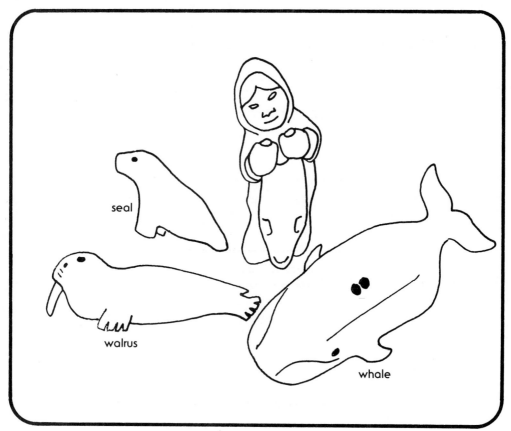

seal

walrus

whale

Across northern Siberia, Alaska, Canada, and Greenland stretches a climate of ice and snow for most of the
year. Nothing grows. It is always cold. But the Eskimos
are able to live there. They have lived in North America

5 at least 28,000 years, and they call themselves Inuit. This word means people, and for thousands of years they thought they were the only people in the world.

Life there is probably the most difficult in the world. People have only the most <u>essential</u> things. But they have (necessary)
10 developed beautiful art because for them art is essential.

The Eskimo artist takes a piece of <u>ivory</u> from a sea animal in his hands. Slowly he turns it, looks at it, and feels it. As he begins carving, he starts to dream. He knows the hidden form of the animal is in the ivory. As
15 the artist dreams and carves, the animal slowly appears. It might be a seal or a whale. It might be a fish or a bird. The Eskimo understands animal forms from a life close to nature. He feels a closeness to the land and to the people and animals that live there. He knows how animals move
20 and how they look when they stand still. He is able to make an ivory or bone animal that catches the feeling of a live one exactly.

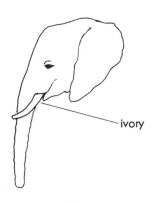
ivory

Why do Eskimos make small animals that cannot be used for anything? Do they have special meaning in their
25 society? Social scientists cannot answer these questions. The Eskimos do not tell them, and they can only guess.

The small animal is not just a copy of a live one. It has something of the animal itself in it. Making the animal is more important than owning it when it is finished. When
30 the artist <u>carves</u> the ivory animal, he understands better (cuts) what it feels like to be an animal.

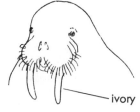
ivory

It is important to the Eskimos to feel and handle the small animal carvings. Handling makes them smooth, and smoothness <u>improves</u> the carvings. Many of the (makes better)
35 animals will not stand up. They fall over and roll around. This is not important. People should hold and feel the carvings, not just look at them.

The small Eskimo carvings of animals, birds, and people are very popular among people who visit north-
40 ern Canada and Alaska. People who cannot visit the area where Eskimos live can see their art in museums. Most of us never see whales or seals, but when we see the beautiful form and color of an ivory or bone animal, we know how beautiful the real animals are.

I. VOCABULARY

society	special	stretches	nature
so	handle	carvings	museums
seal	ivory	essential	Eskimos
smooth	guess	improves	roll
exactly	whale	climate	

1. A climate of ice and snow _____ across North America.
2. _____ are able to live there.
3. Eskimos have only the most _____ things.
4. The artist knows the hidden form of the animal is in the _____.
5. The artist understands animal forms from a life close to _____.
6. It might be a _____ or a _____.
7. The bone animal catches the feeling of a live one _____.
8. Do carvings have a _____ meaning in their society?
9. Social scientists can only _____.
10. It is important to the Eskimo to feel and _____ the small _____.
11. Handling makes them _____.
12. Smoothness _____ the carvings.
13. Many of the animals fall over and _____ around.
14. People can see Eskimo art in _____.

II. VOCABULARY (new context)

stretch	essential	handle	might
smooth	exactly	ivory	roll
climate	carvings	museum	improve
special	guess	whales	nature

1. Some dogs learn to sit up and _____ over.
2. That glass dish is worth $500. Please don't _____ it.
3. A birthday is a very _____ day for children. They usually have a birthday cake and a party.
4. Seals and _____ live in the sea.
5. A glass and a plastic dish are very _____.
6. Can you _____ how old he is? Do you think he is twenty or twenty-five?

7. Canadian English and American English are not _____ the same.
8. How high can you _____ your arms above your head?
9. The government has a new program to _____ the health of village people. They will become healthier.
10. There is a beautiful _____ of Indian art and life in Mexico City.
11. It has hundreds of stone _____.
12. People in the Appalachian Mountains live close to _____.
13. Saudi Arabia has a desert _____. In general, it is hot and dry.
14. It is _____ to heat your house in winter if you live in Canada.

III. VOCABULARY REVIEW

in general	at least	still
service	favorite	toys
earn	equipment	so

1. Her _____ color is green. She likes green best.
2. _____, Newfoundlanders are independent people.
3. Eskimos have made carvings for centuries, and they _____ make them today.
4. The _____ was very slow at our favorite restaurant yesterday, so we left without eating.
5. John received several _____ for his fifth birthday. He played with them for hours.
6. Bring the sports _____ to the picnic so we can play games.
7. An Eskimo artist can _____ a lot of money from his carvings.

IV. ORAL QUESTIONS

1. What kind of climate stretches across northern Alaska and Canada?
2. Why do Eskimos call themselves Inuit?
3. What is life like for the Eskimos?
4. What does an Eskimo do when he starts to make a carving?
5. What animal forms does he often find in the ivory?

6. Why does the artist understand animal forms?
7. Why can he catch the feeling of animals in his carvings?
8. Why do social scientists have to guess about Eskimo art?
9. Which is more important, making the carving or owning it?
10. Why does handling the carvings improve them?
11. What should people do with the carvings?
12. Where can people see Eskimo art?
13. What do we know when we see the animal carvings?

V. COMPREHENSION: True/False/No Information

Write *T* if the sentence is completely true.
Write *F* if it is completely or partly false.
Write *NI* if there is no information about it.

_____ 1. It is very cold in winter in northern Canada, but the summers are very hot.
_____ 2. Art is essential to Eskimos.
_____ 3. Eskimos get ivory from elephants.
_____ 4. Eskimos use small boats to hunt sea animals.
_____ 5. Eskimos make beautiful carvings of animals standing still, but it is too difficult to show how they move.
_____ 6. Eskimos like to explain the meanings of their carvings.
_____ 7. Eskimos paint pictures of animals.

VI. MAIN IDEA

Choose the three main ideas.

_____ 1. Alaska is part of the United States.
_____ 2. Life is difficult for Eskimos, but they still have time for art.
_____ 3. Inuit means people.
_____ 4. An Eskimo carving catches the feeling of a live animal exactly.
_____ 5. Making a carving is more important than owning one.
_____ 6. Most people never see real seals and whales.

WORD STUDY

I. WORD FORMS: -self Pronouns

Singular	Plural
myself	ourselves
yourself	yourselves
herself	themselves
himself	
itself	

NOTE: Most of these use the possessive form: *my, your,* and so on. BUT *himself* and *themselves* use the object form.

Put the correct word in each blank.

1. They call _____ Inuit.
2. Sometimes an Eskimo artist sings to _____ as he makes a carving.
3. The carving has something of the animal _____ in it.
4. I am going to buy a shirt for _____ and one for my son.
5. Did you find _____ in the class picture, Keiko?
6. The exercise was too difficult for us to do by _____. We had to do it in class.
7. She didn't eat at a fast-food restaurant yesterday. She made a sandwich for _____.
8. Speak English among _____, and you will learn faster.

II. NOUN SUBSTITUTES

Example: The Eskimo artist takes a piece of ivory in his hands.
Slowly he turns <u>it</u>. it = a piece of ivory

Look at these words in the reading selection.
Tell what each word means.

1. page 46, line 4   they
2. page 47, line 13   he

3.	line 16	it
4.	line 19	there
5.	line 26	them
6.	line 26	they
7.	line 27	one
8.	line 27	it
9.	line 41	their

III. WORD FORMS

| -ness | | t → ce | |
Adjective	Noun	Adjective	Noun
smooth	smoothness	important	importance
happy	happiness	different	difference
weak	weakness	silent	silence

Add -en to each word to make a verb.

-en (darken = make something dark or darker)

Noun	Verb	Adjective	Verb
strength	_____	dark	_____
length	_____	weak	_____
		wide	_____

Write the correct form of the word in each sentence. Underline all the direct objects.

(smooth) 1. _____ is important, so handling improves the carvings.

(length) 2. These pants are too short. I will have to _____ them.

(different) 3. Modern and traditional clothes are different. Do you understand the _____?

(dark) 4. The paint is not the right color. Put some black paint in to _____ it.

(happy) 5. Fame does not always bring _____.

(silent) 6. You can almost hear the _____ in northern Canada.

(important)   7. Social scientists do not understand the _____
of animal carvings in Eskimo society.

(strength)   8. Running will _____ your legs.

(weak)   9. Abdullah hurt his knee in a soccer game. Now he has a
_____ in that leg.

(wide)   10. The city is going to _____ the street on which
I live.

IV. CONTEXT CLUES

1. A plane going from London to New York flies across the <u>ocean</u>. It takes
several hours.
   a. land with water all around it   c. a large city
   b. a large body of water   d. a large country

2. Mary took her gold <u>necklace</u> from the jewelry box and put it around her
neck. It looked beautiful with her new blue dress.
   a. something small and round to wear on a finger
   b. a kind of watch to wear on the arm
   c. something made of gold to wear on the ears
   d. a kind of jewelry to wear around the neck

3. The mother cat took care of her four <u>kittens</u> until they were old enough
to take care of themselves.
   a. friends   c. food
   b. eyes and ears   d. baby cats

4. My friend didn't want to go to the party because she was very tired.
However, I <u>persuaded</u> her to go, and she had a good time.
   a. invited
   b. guessed the reason
   c. caused someone to do something
   d. improved

5. The dancers <u>whirled</u> faster and faster to the loud music.
   a. turned around and around   c. sang
   b. whiled away   d. ran

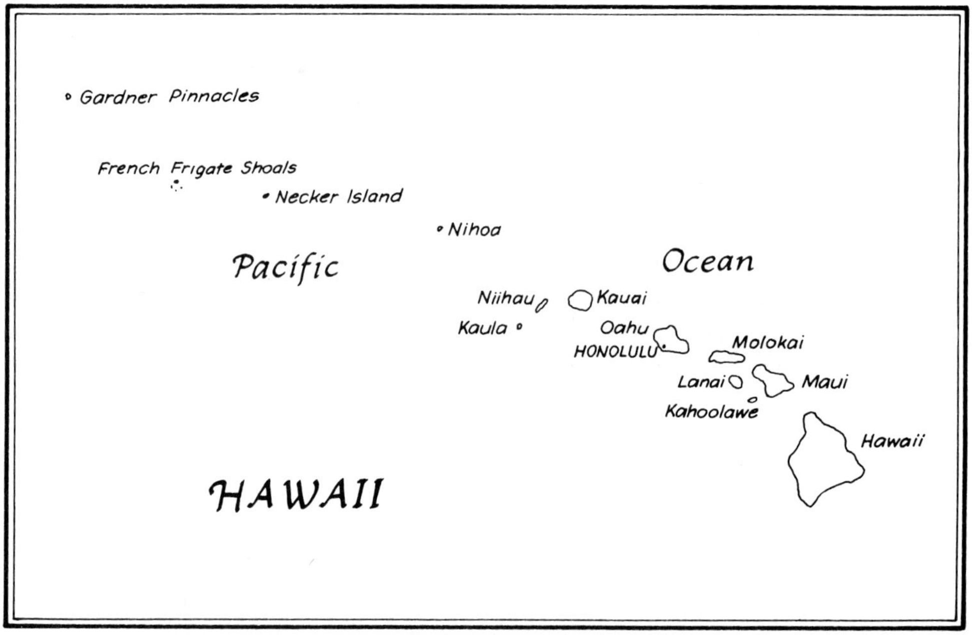

Gardner Pinnacles

French Frigate Shoals

Necker Island

Nihoa

Pacific

Ocean

Niihau

Kauai

Kaula

Oahu

HONOLULU

Molokai

Lanai

Maui

Kahoolawe

Hawaii

HAWAII

HAWAII, ISLAND STATE

Hawaii Visitors Bureau, Honolulu

Out in the Pacific Ocean, 3,700 kilometers from Los Angeles, lies Hawaii, the fiftieth state of the United States. This group of eight main islands has a land area of only 16,700 square kilometers stretched over 2,500 kilometers

5 of ocean. It became a state in 1959 and is smaller than
forty-six other states.

It is strange that this small group of islands, so far from
the U.S. mainland, is a state. But history does strange
things.

10 The first Hawaiians arrived from other Pacific islands
sometime around 100 A.D. Their society developed for
centuries without visitors from Europe, Asia, or Africa.
Then all this changed. In 1778, Captain James Cook, the
great English explorer, visited Hawaii. He put the islands

15 on his maps of the Pacific. Ships <u>searching for</u> whales be-   (looking for)
gan stopping for supplies.

Then in 1820 a small group of people from the eastern
United States came to teach the Hawaiians about Christianity. They started farms to grow sugar and, later, pine-

20 apples. Soon there were not enough people to do all the
farm work, so the farm owners brought in Asians—Chinese
starting in 1852, Japanese in 1868, and Filipinos in 1906.
Koreans, Portuguese, and Puerto Ricans also came. Each
group worked hard, saved their money, and built homes.

25 They got better jobs or started their own small businesses.
More people came from the U.S. mainland and from
other Pacific islands. Hawaii became a society with traditions from several countries.

Today about 800,000 people live in Hawaii, but only

30 about 10,000 are Hawaiian. Another 90,000 are part
Hawaiian. People among the different national groups
have married each other, so today the groups are partly
mixed. A child might have a Chinese-Hawaiian mother
and a Portuguese-Filipino father.

35 There are some special traditions in Hawaii. People
are very friendly and always welcome visitors. They give
visitors a lei, a long necklace of beautiful fresh flowers.
Men wear bright flowered shirts, and women often wear
long flowered dresses. There are traditional Chinese,

40 Japanese and Filipino holidays and all the holidays from
the United States. They call Hawaii the Aloha State.
Aloha means both hello and goodbye. It also means I
love you.

Hawaiians earn most of their money from tourists, and

45 most of the tourists come from the mainland and from
Japan. There are so many people living in Hawaii now
that there are residential areas where there used to be
farms. Some of the big sugar and pineapple companies
have moved to the Philippines, where they do not have
50 to pay workers as much money. The families of the first
people who came from the U.S. mainland own the important banks and companies. Japanese are also buying
or starting businesses.

Usually when people from different countries, races,
55 and traditions live together, there are serious problems.
There are a few problems in Hawaii, but in general people
have learned to live together in peace.

I. VOCABULARY

ocean	pineapples	races	Christianity
necklace	serious	history	holidays
mainland	traditions	searching	mixed

1. Out in the Pacific _____ lies Hawaii, the fiftieth state.
2. _____ does strange things.
3. Ships _____ for whales began stopping for supplies.
4. In 1820 a group of people came to teach the Hawaiians about _____.
5. They started farms to grow sugar and _____.
6. Today the different national groups are partly _____.
7. A lei is a long _____ of fresh flowers.
8. There are traditional Chinese, Japanese, and Filipino _____.
9. People in Hawaii are from different countries, _____, and traditions.
10. Usually when people from different traditions live together, there are _____ problems.

II. VOCABULARY (new context)

Christianity	island	race	stretch
ocean	mix	necklace	serious
explorer	history	holiday	search

1. To make hot chocolate, _____ together milk, chocolate, and sugar.
2. Some people are very _____. They work all the time and do not laugh and enjoy themselves very much.
3. Tomorrow is a _____, so there are no classes.
4. In 1849 people went to California to _____ for gold.
5. You can cross the _____ by ship and plane but not by car.
6. Students study the _____ of their country to learn what happened in the past.
7. Most Europeans belong to the white _____.
8. A silver _____ looks beautiful with a green dress.

III. VOCABULARY REVIEW

Match each word or phrase with the correct meaning. Write the meaning in Column B next to the word in Column A.

A	**B**
1. million	a. necessary
2. imagine	b. quiet
3. essential	c. 1,000,000
4. silence	d. change
5. handle	e. think of
6. human beings	f. quite
7. rearrange	g. hold in the hands
	h. people
	i. ivory

IV. ORAL QUESTIONS

1. Where is Hawaii?
2. Where did the first Hawaiians come from?
3. Why did whaling ships stop at Hawaii?
4. Why did the first people from the U.S. mainland come to Hawaii?
5. Why does Hawaii have different national traditions?
6. What are some of the special traditions?
7. How do Hawaiians earn most of their money?
8. Why did some big sugar and pineapple companies move to the Philippines?
9. Who owns most of the big businesses in Hawaii?
10. Are there serious problems among the different groups of people in Hawaii?

V. COMPREHENSION

1. Hawaii has a land area of _____ square kilometers.
   a. 16,700
   b. 3,700
   c. 2,500
   d. 1,820

*2. Whaling ships learned about Hawaii from _____.
   a. Christians
   b. Captain Cook's maps
   c. Hawaiian seamen
   d. Japanese visitors

*3. _____ came from islands to live in Hawaii.
   a. Portuguese and Koreans
   b. Japanese and Chinese
   c. Japanese and Filipinos
   d. Filipinos and Koreans

4. Today the people from the different national groups are _____.
   a. completely separated
   b. partly mixed
   c. completely mixed
   d. living in different societies

*5. Which one is probably NOT true?
   a. Tourists spend a lot of money in Hawaii.
   b. The people in Hawaii are all Christians.
   c. You can hear country music on the radio in Hawaii.
   d. Hawaii has a warm climate.

VI. COMPREHENSION: Hawaiian Time Line

Find the dates for the events listed below. Put each date in the right place on the line. Write the event under it. The first one is done for you. (The empty space in the line shows a break in it. It would make the line too long to put all the dates on it.)

1. Hawaiians arrived
2. Japanese arrived
3. Christianity arrived
4. Became a state
5. Chinese arrived
6. Captain Cook visited
7. Filipinos arrived

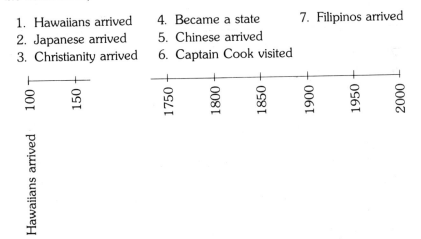

VII. MAIN IDEA

Choose the three main ideas.

_____ 1. Hawaii stretches over 2,500 kilometers of ocean.
_____ 2. Hawaii is a state in the United States.
_____ 3. Hawaii is a society of different races and traditions.
_____ 4. Different groups live together in peace in Hawaii.
_____ 5. Captain Cook was a famous explorer.
_____ 6. The first Japanese came to Hawaii in 1868.

WORD STUDY

I. IRREGULAR VERBS

Present	Past	Past Participle
1. become	became	become
2. drive	drove	driven
3. catch	caught	caught
4. sing	sang	sung
5. choose	chose	chosen
6. mean	meant	meant
7. fall	fell	fallen

Learn the verb forms. Choose the correct form for each blank. Use a word from line 1 in sentence 1, and so on.

1. Hawaii _____ a state in 1959.
2. If you have ever _____ in New York at 5:00 P.M., you know the traffic moves very slowly.
3. Fishing boats have _____ fish off the coast of Newfoundland for centuries.
4. Sometimes the Eskimo artist _____ to himself as he turns the ivory in his hands.
5. The buyer for a store _____ twenty carvings.
6. I _____ to telephone you yesterday, but I forgot.
7. An ivory carving _____ from the table and rolled across the floor.

II. WORD FORMS: Nouns

Use a noun after a preposition. (The preposition *to* is different. There is often a verb after *to*.)

Underline the preposition. Write the noun form in the blank.

-ture		-er		same	
Verb	**Noun**	**Verb**	**Noun**	**Verb**	**Noun**
mix	mixture	explore	explorer	change	change
sign	signature	dry	dryer	work	work
furnish	furniture	wash	washer	start	start

Adjective	**Noun**
strange	stranger

(explore)   1. James Cook is the name of an _____.

(change)   2. The speaker explained the reason for the _____ in the program.

(mix)   3. To make lemonade, mix lemon juice and water. Then add sugar to the _____.

(strange)   4. I talked to a _____ at the party and found out he is from my hometown.

(sign)   5. There is a place for your _____ at the bottom of the page.

(start)   6. Linda was ahead of everyone thirty seconds after the _____ of the race.

(wash, dry)   7. In a half hour would you please take the clothes out of the _____ and put them in the _____?

(furnish)   8. What kind of _____ do you have in your apartment?

(work)   9. What kind of _____ do you do in your country?

III. CONTEXT CLUES

1. <u>Divide</u> this circle into four parts.
   - a. +
   - b. −
   - c. ×
   - d. ÷

2. The population of China is about one billion people.
   a. the money people earn
   b. the number of men in a country
   c. the number of people that live in a place
   d. something everyone likes
3. The two major languages in South America are Spanish and Portuguese. There are also many Indian languages.
   a. most important   c. most difficult
   b. studies   d. social
4. The class includes students from Japan, Libya, and Brazil.
   a. closes   c. studies
   b. has in it   d. does homework
5. The fire bell rang for two minutes. When it ceased, the silence was wonderful.
   a. quiet   c. started
   b. limited   d. stopped
6. It was easier to build railroads across the prairies of Canada than across the mountains.
   a. flat grasslands   c. lakes and rivers
   b. large cities   d. states

LANGUAGE AND LANGUAGES

One of the differences between humans and other animals is that humans have language and other animals do not. Language is human <u>speech</u>, either written or   (noun for speak)
spoken. There are about 3,000 spoken languages in the
5 world, but some are spoken by only a few hundred people.

All languages have (1) a system of sounds, (2) words, (3) a system of word order, and (4) grammar. Word order is more important in English than in some other lan-
10 guages. The sound system is very important in Chinese and in many African languages.

Language is always changing. In a society where life continues year after year with few changes, the language does not change much either. The earliest known lan-
15 guages had complicated grammar but a small, limited vocabulary. Over the centuries, the grammar changed, and the vocabulary grew. For example, the English and Spanish people who came to America during the six-teenth and seventeenth centuries gave names to all the
20 new plants and animals they found. In this way, hundreds of new words were introduced into English and Spanish vocabularies. Today life is changing very fast, and lan-guage is changing fast, too.

There are several <u>major</u> language families in the world.   (main)
25 Some scientists say there are nine main families, but other scientists <u>divide</u> them differently. The languages in   ($\div$)
each family are related, and scientists think that they came from the same parent language. About 3 percent of the people in the world speak languages that are not in
30 these major families.

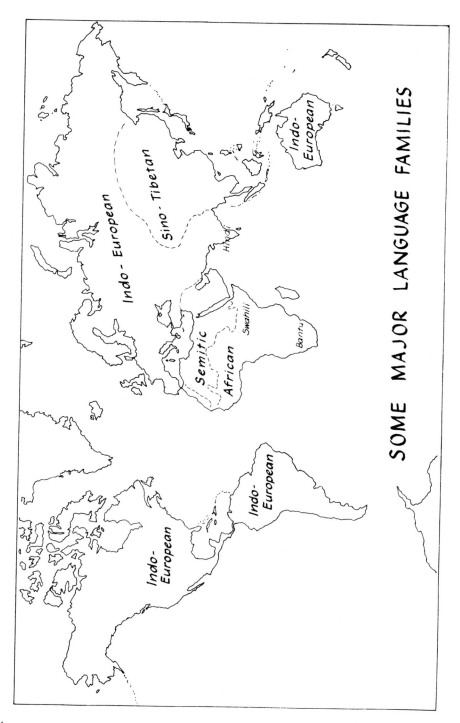

SOME MAJOR LANGUAGE FAMILIES

The largest family is the Indo-European family. About   (Indian)
half of the world's population speaks these languages.
They stretch from northern Europe to India. They are
also spoken in North and South America, Australia, New
35 Zealand, and South Africa. English is one of the Germanic
group of Indo-European languages.

Another group is the Sino-Tibetan family, which in-   (Chinese)
cludes Chinese, Thai, Burmese, and Tibetan. The Semitic
family includes Arabic, Hebrew, and Amharic (the lan-
40 guage of Ethiopia). Scientists are not sure if Japanese and
Korean are in the same family. There are over 1,200
American Indian languages, but they are very difficult to
divide into groups because there are many differences
among them. There are many African languages spoken
45 south of the Sahara Desert. It is also very difficult to divide these into families.

We learn our own language by listening and copying.
We do this without studying or thinking about it. But
learning a foreign language takes a lot of study and
50 practice.

I. VOCABULARY

population	limited	system	differences
speech	sounds	includes	related
major	order	introduced	divide

1. Language is human _____.
2. All languages have a _____ of sounds.
3. They also have a system of word _____.
4. The earliest known languages had a small, _____ vocabulary.
5. Hundreds of new words were _____ into English and
   Spanish.
6. There are several _____ language families in the world.
7. The languages in each family are _____.
8. About half of the world's _____ speaks Indo-European
   languages.

9. The Sino-Tibetan family _____ Chinese and Tibetan.
10. American Indian languages are difficult to _____ into groups.

II. VOCABULARY (new context)

speech	major	system	difference
limited	include	population	divided
human	order	introduce	related

1. John's _____ at the university is electrical engineering.
2. What is the _____ of your country? How many people live there?
3. A soccer team is _____ to eleven players. Only eleven people can play at one time.
4. The education _____ in the United States is a little different from state to state.
5. Ten _____ by two is five.
6. When you write your composition about your country, please _____ information on the education system.
7. The program included a short _____ about the history of country music.
8. Put these numbers in the right _____: 4, 2, 3, 5, 1.
9. Country music is _____ to cowboy music.
10. I would like to _____ you to my parents.

III. VOCABULARY REVIEW: Antonyms

Match each word with the word that means the opposite.

1. traditional
2. complicated
3. exact
4. essential
5. special
6. search
7. educated

a. inexact
b. island
c. simple
d. find
e. unnecessary
f. modern
g. ordinary

8. marry
9. agree
10. city

h. disagree
i. necklace
j. divorce
k. country
l. uneducated

IV. ORAL QUESTIONS

1. What is one of the differences between humans and other animals?
2. What is language?
3. What are four things that all languages have?
4. What is very important in English?
5. In what languages is the sound system very important?
6. What kind of grammar and vocabulary did the earliest languages have?
7. What is happening to language today?
8. What is the largest major family?
9. Where are these languages spoken?
10. What group is English in?
11. Why are American Indian languages difficult to divide into groups?
12. How do we learn our own language?
*13. Name some Indo-European languages.
*14. What families are the languages of Brazil and North Africa in?

V. COMPREHENSION

1. All languages have _____.
   a. large vocabularies
   b. a system of sounds
   c. simple grammar
   d. complicated vocabularies
2. Word order is more important in _____ than in some other languages.
   a. English
   b. Tibetan
   c. Chinese
   d. Spanish
3. The sound system is very important in _____.
   a. Japanese
   b. Chinese
   c. English
   d. Arabic
4. The earliest known languages had _____ grammar.
   a. limited
   b. residential
   c. complicated
   d. imaginable

5. _____ gave hundreds of new words to English and Spanish.
   a. Africa   c. China
   b. Asia   d. America
6. Today there are several major language _____.
   a. families   c. museums
   b. relatives   d. races
7. About _____ of the world's population speaks Indo-European languages.
   a. one-fourth   c. one-fifth
   b. one-third   d. one-half
8. It is difficult to divide American Indian languages into groups because _____.
   a. they are spoken only by Indians
   b. there are many differences among them
   c. they are Indo-European
   d. only 3 percent of the people speak them
*9. _____ is an Indo-European language.
   a. Italian   c. Burmese
   b. Swahili   d. Indonesian
*10. The answer is not in the reading, but it is probably true.
   a. Sound systems and grammar have the same importance in all languages.
   b. Animals can talk.
   c. The use of machines has added many new words to languages.
   d. Some languages are better than others because they have larger vocabularies.

VI. MAIN IDEA

Choose the four main ideas.

_____ 1. Language is human speech.
_____ 2. All languages have a sound system, words, grammar, and a system of word order.
_____ 3. The sound system is important in many African languages.
_____ 4. Language is always changing.
_____ 5. Hundreds of new words were added to Spanish in America.
_____ 6. There are several major language families.

VII. LANGUAGE CHART

Use the reading selection, the language map, and things you already know.
Write these languages in the correct columns.

English	Arabic	Hebrew	Tibetan	Amharic
Thai	Spanish	Burmese	Chinese	Persian
Hindi	Bantu	German	Italian	Portuguese
Swahili				

Indo-European	Sino-Tibetan	Semitic	African

WORD STUDY

I. WORD FORMS: Past Participles as Adjectives

The past participle form of a verb can be used as an adjective. In regular
verbs, the past participle ends in -ed.

Example: limit, limited

Some irregular verbs:

      know, knew, known   speak, spoke, spoken

      write, wrote, written   grow, grew, grown

Write the past participle in each sentence. Underline the noun it describes.

(write)   1. Indo-European languages are _____ languages.

(speak)   2. Some Indian languages are _____ languages,
but they are not written.

(limit)   3. Some languages have a _____ vocabulary.

(make)   4. <u>Home</u> _____ food tastes better than fast food.

(complicate)   5. The earliest known languages had _____
grammar.

(know)   6. Pelé is a well-_____ soccer player.

(eat)   7. There was a glass of milk and a <u>half-</u>_____
apple on the kitchen table.

II. PREPOSITIONS

by = as a result of

    You can learn another language by studying.

Use the -ing form of the verb after a preposition except to.

by plane

by ship

by bus

by car

    They went to Canada <u>by</u> plane.

    Use <u>by</u> when it has only one word after it.

BUT in my car; in a car

    in my friend's car

    on my bicycle

    on the bus

    on foot

        BUT People usually say, "Walk."

           "I come to class on foot" is correct, but people do not
usually say this. They say, "I walk to class."

Use *by, at, in, of,* or *on* in the blanks.

1. She usually comes to the university _____ bus, but sometimes she comes _____ her friend's car.
2. The final exam will be _____ May 16.
3. We learn our own languages _____ listening and copying.
4. Word order is very important _____ English.
5. English is spoken _____ Australia.
6. You can learn a lot _____ watching television.
7. I usually come to class _____ my bicycle, but today I came _____ the bus.
8. Who is that standing _____ the window?
9. There are several major language families _____ the world.
10. One _____ the differences between humans and other animals is language.
11. Have you ever traveled _____ ship?
12. Winter begins _____ three days.
13. The car parked _____ the tree is mine.

III. CONTEXT CLUES

1. This school <u>provides</u> books, but the children must buy their own paper and pencils.
   a. sells   c. teaches
   b. buys   d. supplies
2. Fifty people in the village died of a <u>disease</u>.
   a. sickness   c. easy
   b. health   d. doctor
3. Which of these <u>figures</u> is the largest, 6, 50, or 1,631?
   a. numbers   c. answers
   b. letters   d. ages
4. Life in Canada and the United States is <u>similar</u>. The societies are not very different.
   a. very different   c. modern
   b. almost the same   d. traditional
5. It is <u>common</u> to see horses in cowboy TV programs. There are not usually any horses in police programs.
   a. different   c. important
   b. unpopular   d. usual

6. A car almost hit me when I was riding my bicycle this morning. I <u>prevented</u> an accident by turning quickly into another street.
   a. was careful
   b. made something happen
   c. stopped something before it happened
   d. rode a bicycle on a different street
7. John tried to get on the bus, but it was already <u>overcrowded</u>. He could not even find a place to stand because it was so full of people. He had to wait for the next bus.
   a. above the people
   b. too many people
   c. going in the wrong direction
   d. the wrong bus
8. The population of Mexico City will <u>increase</u> from 15 million to 31 million by the year 2000.
   a. change
   b. include
   c. limit
   d. get larger

THIRD WORLD CITIES

The year 2000 is less than twenty years away, a very short time in the history of the world. But in that short time the world will reach a population of 6.2 billion, almost 2 billion more people than there are today. Unfor-
5 tunately, the greatest growth will be in the cities of the poorest nations.

The population <u>figures</u> seem almost unbelievable.   (numbers)
There will be 60 cities in the world with populations of more than 5 million. Forty-five of them will be in the third
10 world. There will be 22 cities with populations of over 20 million and almost 300 cities with over one million people each. Mexico City will have 31 million people; Tokyo, 24 million; and Cairo, 13 million.

Social scientists say that this is a natural growth. There
15 was a <u>similar</u> population growth as industries developed   (almost the same)
in Europe during the nineteenth century. People moved to cities to get jobs. However, that growth was much slower because of several important differences. Health conditions in European cities were very bad, and people
20 died of many different kinds of <u>disease.</u> Today some of   (sickness)
these diseases are not <u>common</u> or can be prevented.   (usual)
Even in poor cities, health services are better, and people live longer.

In the nineteenth century Europeans could leave their
25 countries to live in the colonies in Africa and Asia. They could move to the new countries in North and South America. Today the colonies are independent, and it is more difficult to move from one country to another.

A century ago people might spend weeks walking or

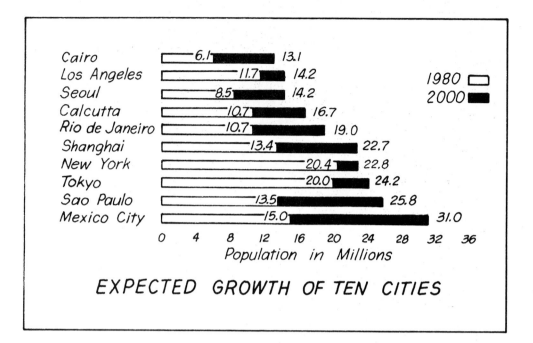

EXPECTED GROWTH OF TEN CITIES

Cairo	6.1	13.1
Los Angeles	11.7	14.2
Seoul	8.5	14.2
Calcutta	10.7	16.7
Rio de Janeiro	10.7	19.0
Shanghai	13.4	22.7
New York	20.4	22.8
Tokyo	20.0	24.2
Sao Paulo	13.5	25.8
Mexico City	15.0	31.0

1980 □ 2000 ■

Population in Millions

Percent of World Population Living in Cities	
1900	5
1950	15
1975	36
2000	50

Number of Cities with a Population Over 5 Million	
1950	6
1980	26
2000	60

30 traveling on an animal to a large city. Today they can go on a bus in only a few hours.

Third world cities are already <u>overcrowded</u>. But city   (too much) workers earn two to ten times as much as people in the country. So thousands of more people arrive every year.
35 The governments must provide electricity, water, schools, health services, and land for houses. But poor countries do not have the money to do this. As cities grow larger, the problems increase.

However, some social scientists believe the problems
40 are not hopeless. People move to cities because they want to change and improve their lives. When they can

find jobs, they work hard. They build nice houses when
they have the money and send their children to school.
These hardworking people help build a better society for
45 the whole country.

I. VOCABULARY

history	increase	common	figures
social	diseases	unfortunately	conditions
prevented	similar	provide	colonies
overcrowded			

1. Twenty years is a short time in the _____ of the world.
2. _____, the greatest growth will be in the cities of the poorest nations.
3. The population _____ seem almost unbelievable.
4. There was a _____ growth as industries developed in Europe.
5. Health _____ in European cities were very bad.
6. People died of many different _____.
7. Today some of these diseases are not _____.
8. Some of them can be _____.
9. Third world cities are already _____.
10. The government must _____ electricity, water, and schools.
11. As cities grow larger, the problems _____.

II. VOCABULARY (new context)

overcrowded	disease	prevent	reach
provides	nations	figures	common
increase	similar	conditions	unfortunately

1. Small towns in Canada and the United States are _____, but towns in Mexico are different.
2. A computer can add and divide _____ faster than any other machine.
3. Country music _____ enjoyment for millions of people.
4. Millions of people in New York live in crowded _____.
5. Divorce is _____ in the United States today.
6. _____, divorce causes problems for children.

7. There is an _____ in the number of divorces in Canada.
8. Drivers must drive carefully to _____ accidents.
9. Heart _____ is the number one killer in many industrial nations.

III. VOCABULARY REVIEW

handle	arrange	armies	guessed
produces	each other	roll over	studios
smartest	separate	realize	controls

1. The _____ students do not always get the best grades.
2. Governments spend millions of dollars to buy equipment for their _____ .
3. Tourists in Los Angeles usually visit Universal _____, where movies are made.
4. Animals cannot talk to _____ with words.
5. Venezuela _____ oil.
6. North and South Korea are two _____ countries.
7. Please _____ these names in alphabetical order.
8. The government _____ industrial development in the Soviet Union.
9. He was late for the country music program because he did not _____ what time it was.
10. María, _____ where the new student was from when she heard him talk.

IV. ORAL QUESTIONS

1. What will the population of the world be in the year 2000?
2. Where will the greatest population growth be?
3. When was there a similar population growth in Europe?
4. Name four ways the growth of European cities in the nineteenth century was different from the growth of third world cities today.
5. Why do people move to cities?
6. What must the government provide for new people in cities?
7. Why do some social scientists believe the problems are not hopeless?
*8. About how many people are there in the world today?

V. COMPREHENSION

Use the reading, the tables, and the graph to answer the questions. Write a short answer at the end of the question.

1. What was the world's largest city in 1980?
2. What will the largest city be in 2000?
3. What percent of the world's people lived in cities in 1950?
4. How many third world cities will have a population over 5 million in 2000?
5. What was Mexico City's population in 1980?
6. What was the increase in the number of cities over 5 million from 1950 to 1980?
7. What will Rio de Janeiro's population be in 2000?
8. In what year did 36 percent of the world's population live in cities?
9. What will the population of the world be in 2000?
10. How many cities will have over a million people in 2000?

VI. MAIN IDEA

Choose the three main ideas.

_____ 1. Third world cities are growing very fast.
_____ 2. There will be forty-five third world cities with a population over 5 million in 2000.
_____ 3. City growth in the twentieth century is different from city growth in the nineteenth century.
_____ 4. There are many problems in third world cities because of the population growth.
_____ 5. People in European cities in the nineteenth century could move to colonies.

WORD STUDY

I. WORD FORMS: VERB + -ing

You can use the -ing form of a verb as a noun.

Example: Teaching is an interesting job.
Tom enjoys studying.

Spelling: 1. When a word ends in silent *e,* drop the *e* before adding *-ing.*
2. When a word has one syllable with one vowel followed by one consonant, double the consonant before adding *-ing.* (This is the 1−1−1 rule.)

swim—swimming   BUT speak—speaking
talk—talking

Write the noun form of each verb.

(swim)   1. _____ is a popular sport.
(watch)   2. He improved his English by _____ TV.
(ski)   3. _____ is a seasonal sport.
(eat)   4. _____ foreign food is popular in London.
(rearrange)   5. Joan made more room on her desk by _____ her books and papers.

II. WORD FORMS: Common noun endings from Lessons 1—8: -ment, -th, -ness, -ce, -ture, -ure, -er, -ity

Verb	Noun	Adjective
1.	similarity	similar
2. crowd	crowd	crowded
3.	Christianity	Christian
4. excel	excellence	excellent
5. pay	payment	
6. equip	equipment	
7.	popularity	popular
8. weaken	weakness	weak
9. please	pleasure	pleasant
10. furnish	furniture	furnished

Choose the correct form of each word. Some nouns may be plural. Use a word from line 1 in sentence 1, and so on.

1. There are several major _____ between Qatar and Kuwait.
2. A _____ of people was waiting outside the movie theater.

3. Most Latin Americans are _____.
4. France is famous for the _____ of its food.
5. They will make monthly _____ on their new car for three years.
6. Sports _____ is usually expensive.
7. Sometimes it is hard to understand the _____ of a new movie star.
8. The major _____ of the health program is this: it will cost too much money.
9. It is always a _____ to see an old friend.
10. How much will it cost to _____ your new apartment?

III. CONTEXT CLUES

1. New York is the <u>location</u> of the tallest buildings in the world.
   a. figure
   b. place
   c. condition
   d. major
2. The child was so <u>frightened</u> by the Frankenstein movie that he would not sleep by himself.
   a. pleased
   b. popular
   c. afraid
   d. happy
3. Farmers plant their <u>crops</u> in the spring. They take care of them all summer, and in the fall they can use the plants for food, clothes, or other things. They can use them themselves or sell them.
   a. plants that a farmer grows
   b. plants that produce vegetables and fruit
   c. plants that grow in the desert
   d. plants that produce cotton and oil
4. Ms. Brown will teach the class today <u>instead of</u> Ms. Baker. Ms. Baker is sick and cannot come to class.
   a. in the place of
   b. with
   c. besides
   d. in front of
5. The Suez <u>Canal</u> is between the Red Sea and the Mediterranean Sea.
   a. a river made by humans
   b. a lake made by humans
   c. an ocean
   d. an island

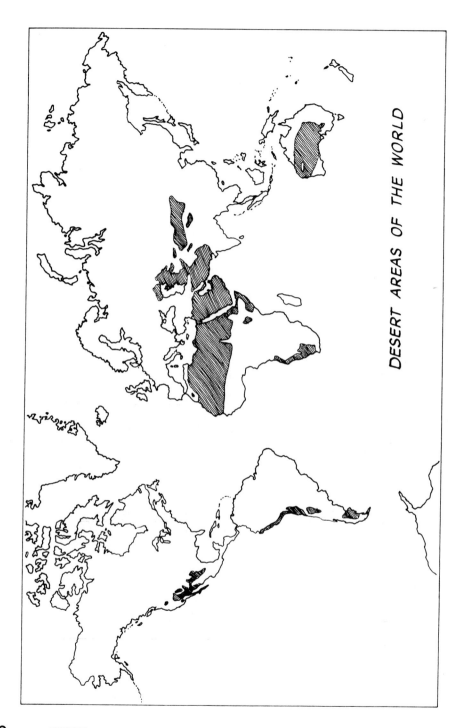

DESERT AREAS OF THE WORLD

DESERTS

Arizona-Sonora Desert Museum, Tucson

A desert is a beautiful land of silence and space. The sun shines, the wind blows, and time and space seem endless. Nothing is soft. The sand and rocks are hard, and many of the plants even have hard <u>needles</u> instead
5 of leaves.

The size and location of the world's deserts are always changing. Over millions of years, as climates change and mountains rise, new dry and wet areas develop. But with-

in the last 100 years, deserts have been growing at a
10 frightening speed. This is partly because of natural
changes, but the greatest desert makers are humans.

In the nineteenth century some of the people living in
the English colonies in Australia got some <u>rabbits</u> from
England. Today there are millions of rabbits that eat
15 every plant in sight. The great desert that covers the center of Australia is growing.

rabbit

The land in the southwestern United States is rich.
Large farms grow crops that need a lot of water, but there
is only a little rainfall. The level of the underground water
20 table is falling every year.

Farming first began in the Tigris-Euphrates Valley, but
today the land there is a desert. In dry areas, people plant
crops on land that is poor and dry. When there are one or
two dry years, the plants die, and the land becomes des-
25 ert. <u>Goats, sheep</u>, and <u>cattle</u> eat every plant they can find.

goat

In developing countries, 90 percent of the people use
wood for cooking and heating. They cut down trees for
firewood. But a tree cools the land under it and keeps the
sun off smaller plants. As the leaves fall, they make the
30 land richer. When the trees are gone, the smaller plants
die, and there is nothing but sand. Yet people must have
firewood, animals, and crops <u>in order to</u> live.

sheep

(to)

Humans can make deserts, but humans can also prevent their growth. Algeria is planting a green wall of trees
35 across the edge of the Sahara to stop the desert sand.
Mauritania is planting a similar wall around Nouakchott,
the capital. Iran puts a thin covering of petroleum on
sandy areas and plants trees. The oil keeps the water and
small trees in the land, and men on motorcycles keep the
40 sheep and goats away. The USSR and India are building
long canals to bring water to desert areas.

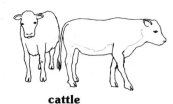

cattle

<u>Yet</u> land that will probably become desert in the future
equals the size of Australia, the USSR, and the United
States together. Can people stop the growth of the world's
45 deserts and save the land that is so essential to life? No
one has the answer.

(however)

I. VOCABULARY

cattle   location   sheep   instead of
rabbits   crops   needles   in order to
frightening   yet   canals   level

1. Many desert plants have hard _____.
2. They have needles _____ leaves.
3. The size and _____ of deserts are always changing.
4. Within the last 100 years, deserts have been growing at a _____ speed.
5. Some people living in Australia got some _____.
6. The _____ of the water table in the southwestern United States is falling every year.
7. People plant _____ on land that is poor and dry.
8. Goats, _____, and _____ eat every plant they can find.
9. People must have firewood, animals, and crops _____ live.
10. The USSR and India are building long _____ to bring water to desert areas.
11. _____ land that will probably become desert in the future equals the size of Australia, the USSR, and the United States together.

II. VOCABULARY (new context)

yet   goats   sheep   rabbit
in general   crops   location   frightening
canal   needle   instead of   in order to
cattle   climate   level   speed

1. Cowboys work with _____ in the western United States.
2. Please tell the _____ of the industrial cities in your country. Where are they?
3. While Ms. Wagner was making a dress, she dropped her _____ and could not find it.
4. In the highest _____ English class, the students give speeches.
5. People came to Newfoundland _____ fish.
6. The Panama _____ goes from the Atlantic to the Pacific Ocean.

7. Two important _____ in Central America are bananas and coffee.
8. Today many Newfoundlanders work in the paper industry _____ fishing.
9. _____, _____, and _____ are animals.
10. Movies about Dracula are _____.
11. Life is difficult in third world cities _____ people continue to move there.

III. VOCABULARY REVIEW

necklace	provide	special	instead of
so	serious	divide	holiday
include	limit	mix	system

1. There is a _____ menu for children in some restaurants.
2. People cut down trees _____ they can burn the wood for cooking.
3. Independence Day on July 4 is an important _____ in the United States.
4. David is very _____ about his classes. He studies a lot and does not go out very much.
5. Oil and water do not _____.
6. Helen wore earrings and a _____ with her long dress.
7. The _____ of government in Venezuela and the United States is similar.
8. If we do not _____ our use of petroleum, we will not have enough for the future.
9. If you _____ the cake into sixteen pieces, there will be enough for everyone.
10. The price of this car does not _____ the state tax.

IV. ORAL QUESTIONS

1. Describe a desert.
2. What makes the size and location of deserts change?
3. How is the size of deserts changing today?

4. What happened to make the size of the Australian desert increase?
5. Why is the level of the water table falling in the southwestern United States?
6. How do animals and farming cause deserts to grow?
7. Why do deserts grow when people cut down trees?
8. Describe the government programs to prevent the growth of deserts in five countries.

V. COMPREHENSION: True/False/No Information (T/F/NI)

_____ 1. In general, desert plants have large, beautiful flowers.
_____ 2. Space seems to have no limit in the desert.
_____ 3. The size of deserts has changed greatly in the past 100 years, but it did not change before that.
_____ 4. Most people in developing countries cook on wood fires.
_____ 5. Elephants help make deserts.
_____ 6. Australia was once an English colony.
_____ 7. Farmers in the southwestern United States grow crops that need just a little water because the climate is dry.
_____ 8. Farming started in the Tigris-Euphrates Valley, and now the area is a desert.
_____ 9. Algeria is planting a wall of trees to keep the cattle away.
_____ 10. Russia is building a canal to bring water to a desert area.
_____ 11. The size of the world's deserts will probably increase before people stop the growth.

VI. MAIN IDEA

Read the two main ideas of this lesson that are written below. Put the letters of the supporting ideas under the correct main idea. Three of them do not belong in either column.

Main Ideas

1. Humans make deserts.   2. Humans can stop the growth of deserts.

a. Algeria is planting a green wall to stop the Sahara.
b. A desert is a beautiful land of silence and space.

c. English people brought rabbits to Australia.
d. People cut down trees for firewood.
e. India is building a canal to a desert area.
f. Many desert plants have needles.
g. Goats, sheep, and cattle eat every plant they can find.
h. Iran puts petroleum on sandy areas and plants trees.
i. Rocks are hard.

WORD STUDY

I. SUFFIXES: -less

-less = not having, without

There is an *endless* number of English words to learn. (There is no end to the number of words.)

Add *-less* to each word. Then use the correct word in each sentence.

care	end	worth	thought
hope	help	change	sleep

1. Time and space in the desert seem _____.
2. Problems in third world cities are not _____.
3. Babies cannot take care of themselves. Someone must help them because they are _____.
4. This is not a diamond. It is only glass. It is _____.
5. Life in some villages is _____. It is the same as it was a century ago.
6. Your composition is good, but it has too many _____ mistakes. You have to be more careful.
7. David was sick last night and could not sleep well. He was very tired after a _____ night.
8. Helen said something that hurt my feelings, but she was just not thinking. It was just a _____ mistake.

II. WORD FORMS

1. Use a noun after an article (a, an, the). There may be an adjective before the noun.

   Examples: A desert is a beautiful land of silence and space.
   The population of China is about one billion.

2. Some common noun endings are -sion, -tion, -ation, and -t.

Write the correct word form in each blank. Use the right verb tense and singular or plural nouns. Underline each article and the noun that follows it.

Verb	**Noun**
1. divide	division
2. introduce	introduction
3. explore	exploration
4. educate	education
5. prevent	prevention
6. populate	population
7. complicate	complication
8. inform	information
9. produce	product
10. fly	flight

1. Children learn to do long _____ in math class.
2. Europeans _____ several new diseases to America.
3. The sixteenth century was the Age of _____.
4. Parents want to _____ their children in good schools.
5. People live longer today because of the _____ of many diseases.
6. What is the _____ of the world?
7. The changes in modern societies cause many _____ in family life.
8. The flight from New York will be late. We will _____ you when it arrives.
9. What are the most important _____ of Hawaii?
10. What time does your _____ leave?

III. CONTEXT CLUES

1. Cows, sheep, elephants, and rabbits are <u>mammals</u>. Codfish and bluebirds are not.
    a. animals that give milk
    b. animals that are born alive and drink milk from the mother's body
    c. animals that live in water and can swim
    d. animals that humans use for food or clothing
2. My hair is dirty. I have to buy some <u>shampoo</u> so I can wash it.
    a. a kind of comb for combing the hair
    b. something to use when taking a shower
    c. something similar to soap for washing the hair
    d. a kind of oil to make the hair shiny
3. Mr. Williams planted his first vegetable garden yesterday. He worked all day putting seeds in the ground. Last night he had a <u>pain</u> in his back.
    a. hurt   c. shirt
    b. seed   d. paint
4. Marie is going to Europe this summer. She will fly from Quebec to Montreal. Then she will get an <u>international</u> flight from Montreal to Paris.
    a. between two or more countries
    b. inside one country
    c. between two or more cities
    d. across the ocean
5. There is a national <u>conference</u> on the family in New York. Social scientists will come from every state to meet and talk about family problems.
    a. a speech about a special subject
    b. a meeting of several families
    c. a class about social science
    d. a meeting on a special subject
6. <u>Smoking is not allowed</u> in the classroom. You can smoke in the hall.
    a. You can smoke.
    b. You cannot smoke.
    c. Smoking is bad for you.
    d. Smoking is unpleasant.
7. Pierre was standing on the crowded bus. When it went around a corner, he almost fell down. He <u>grabbed</u> the seat beside him.
    a. cut   c. took hold of
    b. fell on   d. sat down on

SAVE THE WHALES

The Whale Protection Fund, Center for Environmental Education, Washington, D.C.

It is a beautiful day on the Pacific Ocean. Suddenly a long gray shape breaks out of the water, travels a short way, and disappears into the ocean again. Two minutes later it appears again and then disappears. It is a whale
5 swimming from the cold waters of the Arctic Ocean to a warmer place to <u>bear</u> her young.   (give birth to)

harpoon

SAVE THE WHALES

Whales are the largest animals in the world. The gray whale can be up to fifteen meters long and weigh thirty-five tons. The largest whale is the blue whale, which is
10 larger than thirty elephants. A newborn baby weighs two tons and is over eight meters long.

Whales live in the ocean, but they are not fish. They are warm-blooded mammals and must have air to breathe. The babies are born alive and drink milk from the
15 mother's body. It took millions of years for the whale to develop as it is today.

Every spring groups of whales swim hundreds of kilometers to warm places to bear their young. Each group goes to the same place every year. The mothers take very
20 good care of their babies. The adults are very gentle and playful with each other and with humans. They "talk"[1] to each other with a high noise that sounds like singing. This "talking" can be heard for more than 300 kilometers in open area waters.

25 Yet humans kill over a hundred whales a day. They kill them to make perfume, soap, shampoo, animal feed, and industrial oils. Killing them is a modern business with factory ships, helicopters, and harpoons that explode inside the whale. The whale dies very slowly in great pain.   (hurt)
30 Some ships kill every whale they can find, even the mothers and babies. Then there are no young whales to grow up and bear more young.

For several years, millions of people all over the world have been working together to save the whales. In 1979
35 the countries that hunt whales made two important agreements. The Indian Ocean was made a safe place for the animals with no hunting allowed. Factory ships can hunt only in the Antarctic Ocean. At an international conference, the United Nations decided to stop all killing of
40 whales. But ten countries still hunt them—Chile, Cyprus, Denmark, Iceland, Japan, Norway, Peru, Russia, South Korea, and Spain. Of these countries, Japan and Russia kill more than 70 percent of all the whales that are killed.

It is not necessary to kill whales. There are other prod-

[1] "talk"—The quotation marks (" ") show that whales cannot really talk but do something similar.

45 ucts to use instead of whale oil and meat. If the killing
continues, this wonderful animal, which took millions of
years to develop, will be gone. In only a few years there
will be no more whales in the world.

I. VOCABULARY

shampoo	conference	pain	breathe
mammals	bear	international	harpoons
gentle	newborn	perfume	helicopters
explode	allowed		

1. Whales are warm-blooded _____.
2. They must have air to _____.
3. Every spring whales swim to warm places to _____ their young.
4. Humans kill whales to make _____ and _____.
5. They use factory ships and _____.
6. They use _____ that _____ inside the whale.
7. The whale dies very slowly in great _____.
8. The Indian Ocean is a safe place for whales with no hunting _____.
9. At an international _____, the United Nations decided to stop all killing of whales.

II. VOCABULARY (new context)

helicopters	international	conference	perfume
shampoo	breathing	mammals	harpoon
pain	allow	bear	exploded

1. Stamps for _____ mail cost more than stamps for mail within the country.
2. Fish live in water, and most _____ live on land.
3. The police use _____ to help control traffic in large cities. They can see accidents and locations with heavy traffic.
4. Some women like to wear _____ made from roses.
5. The runners were all _____ hard when the race finished.

6. Some gas _____, and there was a bad fire at a gas station last week.
7. Marco had a _____ in his leg for three days after he fell during a basketball game.
8. Three teachers will be absent tomorrow. They are going to a national _____ for English teachers.
9. Most _____ has a little perfume in it so it smells good.
10. The Bakers do not _____ their children to watch TV until their homework is done.

III. VOCABULARY REVIEW

Underline one word that does not belong with the others.

1. rabbit, goat, codfish, cattle
2. prevention, equipment, popularity, grow
3. mall, supermarket, shoe store, department store
4. minute, percent, century, month
5. uncomplicated, easy, simple, difficult
6. bigger, explorer, stranger, owner
7. rainfall, underground, possibility, firewood

IV. ORAL QUESTIONS

1. Are whales fish?
2. Why do they swim to warm places in the spring?
3. Why do humans kill whales?
4. What did the whale-hunting nations agree to in 1979?
5. What did the United Nations decide?
6. Why is it unnecessary to kill whales?
7. What will happen if the killing continues?

V. COMPREHENSION

In this lesson the author is trying to persuade you to believe something. She does this in the two following ways.

1. She gives facts. What sentences give information that shows whales should not be killed?

2. She plays on your feelings. What sentences make you feel bad about killing whales?

Does the author give both sides of the question?

Lesson 5 is about the changes in family life in the Western world. Some people believe very strongly in a traditional family. They think that a man and woman should stay married all their lives. They believe that a wife should not work outside the house. She should take care of her husband, her children, and the house.

Read Lesson 5 again.

Is the author trying to persuade you to believe something about family life? Can you find sentences that show what the author believes?

These are two different kinds of writing. Lesson 5 gives information. Lesson 11 tries to persuade you to believe something. Where do you usually find the kind of writing in Lesson 11?

VI. MAIN IDEA

Choose the one main idea of this lesson.

——————— 1. Whales are wonderful animals.
——————— 2. All killing of whales should be stopped.
——————— 3. Only ten countries kill whales.

WORD STUDY

I. PREFIXES: over-

over- = too much, too many

Third world cities are already <u>overcrowded</u>. They have too many people.

Add *over-* to each word. Then choose the correct word for each sentence.

populated	weight	slept
eat	heated	cooked

1. There are too many people on the island of Java in Indonesia. Java is _____.
2. We were driving in the mountains on a hot day, and our car _____. We had to stop and wait for it to cool down.
3. Waiter, this steak is _____. I asked for rare, and it is well-done.
4. Martin _____ this morning. He has a 9:00 class, but he did not wake up until 9:15.
5. If you _____ every day, you will soon be _____. Eating too much makes you fat.

II. IRREGULAR VERBS

Learn these verb forms. Choose the correct form for each blank. Use verb 1 in sentence 1, verb 2 in sentence 2, and so on.

Present	Past	Past Participle
1. bear	bore	born
2. drink	drank	drunk
3. swim	swam	swum
4. blow	blew	blown
5. shine	shone	shone
6. rise	rose	risen
7. write	wrote	written

Spelling: <u>Writing</u> has one <u>t</u>. writ¢—writing

1. When were you _____?
2. They _____ a lot of water during their trip through the desert last week.
3. Last year she _____ every day, but this year she is too busy.
4. The wind _____ down our biggest tree last night.
5. The sun has _____ every day this week.

6. The sun _____ at 7:18 this morning.

7. How many letters have you _____ since you arrived?

III. NOUN SUBSTITUTES

Look at these words in the reading selection.
Tell what each word means.

1. page 89 line 4   it   5.   line 18   their
2.   line 6   her   6.   line 28   that
3. page 91 line 9   which   7.   line 40   them
4.   line 12 they

IV. CONTEXT CLUES

1. Ms. Davis planted some <u>bushes</u> in front of her house. They will grow to be about one meter high.
   a. tall trees   c. grass
   b. low plants   d. places to walk

2. In the fall farmers <u>gather</u> apples from their apple trees.
   a. buy   c. pick
   b. plant   d. together

3. When scientists develop a new kind of medicine, they test it in <u>experiments</u> with animals. Then they know if it is safe for humans.
   a. tests of something new
   b. experiences
   c. medicine
   d. farms that have animals but no plants

4. There is not any milk for our coffee. I <u>used up</u> all the milk this morning when I made a cake.
   a. used it for a short time   c. picked up
   b. put it in the coffee   d. used all of it

5. The speed limit on main streets is fifty kilometers <u>per</u> hour.
   a. before, within   c. miles
   b. a, an, in each one   d. speed

6. Students should come to class every day <u>unless</u> they are sick. They can stay home if they are not well.
   a. under
   b. even if
   c. except if
   d. less
7. <u>Although</u> it is cold, we will have the picnic.
   a. It is cold, but we will have the picnic.
   b. It is cold, so we will not have the picnic.
   c. We will not have the picnic because it is cold.
   d. It was cold, but we had the picnic.

OIL FROM PLANTS

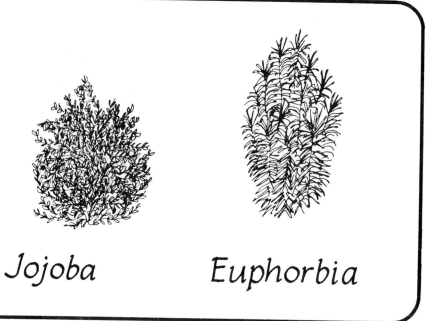

Jojoba   *Euphorbia*

JOJOBA[1]

Whales are fast disappearing from the earth. But surprisingly, they may be saved by a desert plant that is less than a meter high. The jojoba plant is a bush that grows only in southern California, in southern Arizona, and on
5 the west coast of Mexico. The hard fruit of the jojoba contains oil that can be used instead of whale oil. It is already

[1] *Jojoba* is a Spanish word pronounced ho-hó-bah.

being used in shampoo and lipstick. It can be used as an industrial oil, too. It may be possible to use the fruit to make animal feed.

10   For centuries Indians in Arizona have gathered the jojoba fruit. They use the oil to put on burns, to make their hair shine, and to make a drink similar to coffee. Now scientists have planted experimental crops. They say that Indians and other people can earn money from jojoba
15 farming.

    Although the jojoba grows naturally only in the Arizona-Sonora Desert, it can be planted in most dry areas of the world. It needs very little water and can grow on poor land. Jojoba farms could not only produce oil but could
20 also help stop the growth of deserts. And this plant that can grow in the deserts of the world may save a mammal that lives in the sea.

EUPHORBIA[2]

    Petroleum is essential to the modern world. It is burned for energy in cars, homes, and factories. But the world
25 supplies are being used up very fast. Petroleum comes from plants that died millions of years ago. Would it be possible to take oil directly from plants and use it instead of petroleum?

    Scientists think this may be possible with a plant called
30 euphorbia. It grows wild in many areas of the world. Like the jojoba, it can grow on poor land with only a little water. There are experimental euphorbia farms in several countries, and scientists are developing plants from seeds gathered in different places. They think that when the
35 plants are improved enough, they will be able to produce sixty-five <u>barrels</u> of oil per <u>hectare</u> per year.

(10,000 square meters)

    If the experiments are successful, euphorbia farms could provide about 10 percent of the petroleum needs in the United States. Even more important, developing
40 countries could grow euphorbia on their land that is too poor for anything else. Then they would not have to buy expensive petroleum for their energy needs.

[2] *Euphorbia* is pronounced you-fór-be-ah.

I. VOCABULARY

barrels	bush	out	directly
contains	experimental	hectare	seeds
up	energy	although	lipstick
per	gathered		

1. The jojoba plant is a _____ that grows in southern California, in southern Arizona, and on the west coast of Mexico.
2. The hard fruit of the jojoba _____ oil.
3. The oil is already being used in shampoo and _____.
4. For centuries Indians have _____ the jojoba fruit.
5. Now scientists have planted _____ crops.
6. _____ the jojoba grows naturally only in the Arizona-Sonora Desert, it can be planted in most dry areas of the world.
7. Petroleum is burned for _____ in cars, homes, and factories.
8. But the world supplies are being used _____ very fast.
9. Would it be possible to take oil _____ from plants?
10. Scientists are developing plants from _____ from different places.
11. They think the plants will be able to produce sixty-five _____ _____ hectare.

II. VOCABULARY (new context)

directly	lipstick	bushes	per
although	barrels	contains	energy
used up	seeds	experimenting	hectare

1. Rabbits eat leaves and _____ of plants.
2. If you run ten kilometers, your body uses a lot of _____.
3. _____ I should study tonight, I'm going to the movies.
4. Many women wear _____ to make their lips look redder.
5. She earns $10 _____ hour.
6. I've _____ all my paper. Can I borrow some from you?
7. Son, please come _____ home from school. Don't stop to play.

8. Desert countries are _____ with several ways to stop the growth of deserts.

9. Coffee grows on _____.

III. VOCABULARY REVIEW

Match the words with their meanings.

1. instead of	a. to
2. similar	b. everywhere
3. in order to	c. not simple
4. essential	d. in place of
5. realize	e. explode
6. all over	f. know
7. improve	g. hurt
8. complicated	h. like
9. allow	i. conference
10. pain	j. let
	k. necessary
	l. get better

IV. ORAL QUESTIONS

1. How can the jojoba plant possibly save the whales?
2. Where does the jojoba grow naturally?
3. Under what conditions can the jojoba grow?
*4. The population of the world is growing very fast. What effect will this have on the world supply of petroleum?
5. Where does the euphorbia plant grow wild?
6. How is the euphorbia similar to the jojoba?
7. In what way does euphorbia offer hope for the future of developing countries?
*8. How could euphorbia help stop the growth of deserts?

V. COMPREHENSION

1. The jojoba _____.
   a. is a low plant
   b. is a tall plant
   c. grows naturally in many countries
   d. grows in hot wet countries

2. The Arizona-Sonora Desert covers parts of _____ countries.
   a. one   c. three
   b. two   d. several
3. The _____ of the jojoba contains oil.
   a. seed   c. leaf
   b. fruit   d. root
4. The jojoba plant can grow _____.
   a. only in Arizona, California, and Mexico
   b. only on experimental farms
   c. on poor land if it has a lot of water
   d. on poor land with very little water
5. Petroleum provides _____ for the modern world.
   a. factories   c. barrels
   b. energy   d. hectares
6. The euphorbia grows wild _____.
   a. in many areas of the world
   b. only in Arizona, California, and Mexico
   c. on experimental farms
   d. only where deserts are growing
*7. Which one is probably NOT true?
   a. Scientists in different countries work together to find new uses for plants.
   b. In ten years the United States will provide for all its energy needs from plants.
   c. The development of new uses for plants often has other good effects too.
   d. Someday scientists will find other plants with new uses.

VI. MAIN IDEA

Choose the two main ideas.

_____ 1. Scientists are experimenting with oil-producing plants.
_____ 2. Whales are fast disappearing from the earth.
_____ 3. Both the jojoba and euphorbia can grow in a desert climate where most crops cannot grow.
_____ 4. There are experimental euphorbia farms in several countries.

I. SUFFIXES: -ly Adverbs

adj. + *ly* = adverb. An adverb describes a verb.

Usually there are no spelling changes.

usual + ly = usually; complete + ly = completely
BUT: Drop the -le on words ending in -ble.
    possible + ly = possibly
    Change a final *y* to *i*.
    busy + ly = busily.

Write the adverb beside each adjective. Then choose the correct adverb for each blank. Underline the verb it describes.

accidental	silent	similar
inexpensive	thoughtless	possible
careful	easy	

1. It is not hard to swim. You can learn it _____.
2. He _____ told his friend that he did not like the color of her new car. Then he was sorry for what he had said.
3. Always read the directions _____ before you do an exercise.
4. Everything was still as the small Eskimo boat moved _____ through the water.
5. She _____ knocked her glass off the table, and it broke.
6. They plan to live as _____ as possible. They will rent a small apartment and cook their own food.

II. WORD FORMS: Other -ly words

The meaning of a *few* common *-ly* words is different from what you might guess.

1. likely = probable
   The sky is full of gray clouds. It is likely to rain.
   (It will probably rain. It is probable.)
2. greatly = very much
   Family life has changed greatly in two centuries.
   (It has changed very much.)
3. largely = mostly, mainly
   Shopping centers have developed largely because of traffic problems and city growth.
   (They have developed mostly because of traffic and growth.)
4. lately = recently
   I talked to María two weeks ago, but I haven't seen her lately.
   (I haven't seen her recently—not since two weeks ago.)
5. hardly = not much, only a little, almost none
   (Hardly is a negative word. Don't use not or no with it.)
   We have so much homework that we hardly have any time to enjoy ourselves.
   (We have almost no time to enjoy ourselves.)
6. widely = in many places, over a large area
   English is widely used as a second language. Italian is not.
   (English is used in many places.)
7. shortly = in a short time, very soon
   I will finish my homework shortly. Then I can play tennis with you.
   (I will finish very soon.)
8. nearly = almost
   It is nearly 6:00, and we are nearly there.
   (It is 5:55, and we are driving to Chicago. It is almost 6:00, and we are almost there.)

Choose one of the eight words for each sentence.

1. We are _____ to Baltimore. We have just ten more miles to go.
2. She _____ enjoyed the international dance program. It was excellent.
3. Dr. Carter will be with you _____. Please wait just a few minutes.
4. We _____ ever eat in a fast-food restaurant. We usually eat at home.

5. Country music is _____ to be popular for a long time. It will probably be popular twenty years from now.
6. Euphorbia is not a _____-known plant. People in most places have never heard of it.
7. Deserts are growing _____ because of humans and their animals.
8. I used to go to the movies a lot, but I haven't been _____.

III. CONTEXT CLUES

1. What is the <u>solution</u> to this math problem: $12 \div 6 + 8 - 5$?
   a. problem
   b. question
   c. division
   d. answer
2. Did you <u>solve</u> the problem in the first question?
   a. find the answer
   b. ask a question
   c. experiment
   d. locate
3. Grass is not <u>suitable</u> food for humans.
   a. something to wear
   b. easy to grow
   c. right or good
   d. inexpensive
4. The jojoba grows in a dry climate. <u>Nevertheless</u>, it must have some water.
   a. however
   b. unless
   c. instead
   d. essential
5. The <u>buffalo gourd</u> grows wild in the Arizona-Sonora Desert. It is not necessary to plant it.
   a. a kind of animal
   b. a kind of Indian
   c. a kind of plant
   d. a relative of euphorbia
6. It does not matter <u>whether</u> you come in the morning or in the afternoon. You can come anytime.
   a. if
   b. why
   c. climate
   d. where

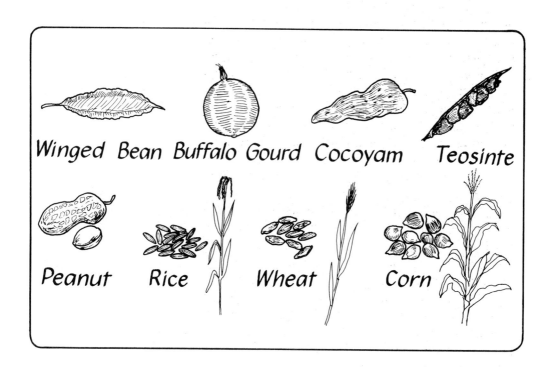

Winged Bean · Buffalo Gourd · Cocoyam · Teosinte

Peanut · Rice · Wheat · Corn

"NEW"[1] PLANTS

As the world's population increases, countries must produce more food. However, deserts are growing, and millions of people are building houses on land that used to be farms. How can we solve a problem that seems to
5 have no <u>solution</u>?   (answer)

One way is to start eating different plants. There are 350,000 kinds of plants in the world. Of these, 80,000 are suitable for humans. But today over one-half of all human food energy and protein comes from corn, wheat,
10 and rice. It is common in developing countries for people to depend on only one or two plants for their food. A disease or bad weather can destroy these crops, and the people have nothing to eat.

Corn, wheat, and rice are between 8 percent and 14
15 percent protein. Meat and fish are from 20 percent to 30 percent protein. Soybeans are almost 40 percent protein. They are an important food in China and Japan. Other beans eaten widely in Latin America have about the same amount of protein as meat.

20 However, there are other plants that are rich in protein. People in parts of Papua-New Guinea and Southeast Asia eat winged beans. They are over 30 percent protein. The marama bean, as rich as the soybean, grows wild in the Kalahari Desert in southern Africa.

25 The potato, an important food in Europe and North America, will not grow in a hot climate. But the cocoyam, similar to the potato, is eaten in Latin America and West

[1] The quotation marks (" ") show that they are not really new plants. They are "new" only because they are not well-known or widely used in the world.

Africa. It can grow in a hot climate, and it does not matter <u>whether</u> the climate is wet or dry.   (if)

30   Scientists are growing crops of buffalo gourds in Mexico and Lebanon. The seeds are up to 35 percent protein. The plant grows wild in the Arizona-Sonora Desert and can grow in other dry areas.

      In 1977 a new kind of teosinte[2] plant was discovered
35 in the mountains of Mexico. It is a relative of corn, but it can probably grow in a wetter climate than corn. Even more important, the teosinte can produce crops every year. They do not have to be replanted from seeds as corn does.

40   <u>Nevertheless</u>, there may be a different kind of problem   (however) with "new" plants. Will people eat different foods? Food is a very important part of our lives, and it is often difficult to change to a different kind of food. However, scientists are hopeful. In the 1920s, George Washington
45 Carver started experimenting with the peanut, which is as rich in protein as meat. He developed many ways to use the peanut as food, and today it is eaten all over the world. Perhaps in a few years the teosinte and the marama bean will be as widely used as the peanut.

I. VOCABULARY

wheat	winged	protein	solve
solution	soybeans	amount	beans
buffalo	peanut	suitable	nevertheless
depend	whether	corn	rice

1. How can we _____ the problem of producing more food?
2. This problem seems to have no _____.
3. About 80,000 plants are _____ food for humans.
4. Today over one-half of all human food energy and _____
   comes from _____, _____, and wheat.
5. Corn, _____, and rice are between 8 percent and 14 percent protein.

[2] Pronunciation: tay-oh-sín-tay.

6. However, _____ are almost 40 percent protein.
7. Other _____ eaten widely in Latin America have about the same amount of protein as meat.
8. People in parts of Papua-New Guinea and Southeast Asia eat _____ beans.
9. Scientists are growing crops of _____ gourds in Mexico and Lebanon.
10. _____, there may be a different kind of problem with new plants.
11. George Washington Carver developed many ways to use the _____.
12. It does not matter _____ the climate is wet or dry for the cocoyam.

II. VOCABULARY (new context)

whether	corn	depend	wheat
wings	rice	solution	protein
solve	beans	suitable	wild
nevertheless	peanut		

1. _____ is a very common food in Asia, Africa, and Latin America.
2. Jeans and a T-shirt are not _____ clothes for dinner at an expensive restaurant.
3. Nadia worked for three hours trying to _____ a problem for her electrical engineering class.
4. The UN decided to stop the killing of whales. _____, ten countries still hunt them.
5. _____ is essential for good health. It is found in meat, fish, beans, milk, seeds, and other foods.
6. A few nations are killing all the whales. What is the _____ to this problem?
7. The _____ of an airplane hold it up in the air.
8. Humans eat many kinds of _____ and rice. These are the seeds of plants.
9. White bread is made from _____.
10. People like to eat pop _____ when they go to a movie.
11. He asked me _____ I wanted tea or coffee.
12. _____ butter is popular with children in the United States.

III. VOCABULARY REVIEW: Synonyms

Choose the word that means the same.

1. likely	a. similar
2. use up	b. probable
3. bear	c. mostly
4. lately	d. not early
5. allow	e. finish
6. largely	f. give birth
7. smart	g. recently
	h. let
	i. intelligent

IV. ORAL QUESTIONS

1. How many plants are suitable for people to eat?
2. What plants provide more than half of human energy and protein?
3. What is a serious problem for a country that depends on one food crop?
*4. Which is richer in protein, rice or beans?
5. Which new plants can grow in desert areas?
*6. Scientists hope to use the teosinte to improve corn plants. How could this save money for farmers?
7. Do people start eating different food easily?
*8. Some people do not eat meat because of their beliefs. How do they get the necessary protein?

V. COMPREHENSION: True/False

_____ *1. As cities grow, they take farmland away from food production.
_____ 2. Humans use most of the plants suitable for food.
_____ 3. Soybeans have more protein than wheat.
_____ 4. The marama bean is as rich in protein as the soybean.
_____ 5. The Kalahari Desert is in the Middle East.
_____ *6. The potato will probably become a common food in Indonesia.
_____ 7. Corn has to be replanted every year.
_____ *8. Foreign students often do not like the food in the country where they study.

VI. COMPREHENSION

Put these names of food in the correct column: buffalo gourd, cocoyam, corn, fish, marama bean, meat, peanut, potato, rice, soybean, teosinte, wheat, winged bean.

PROTEIN IN FOOD

Under 20 Percent	20–30 Percent	30–40 Percent	No Information

VII. MAIN IDEA

Choose the two main ideas in the reading.

_____ 1. People eat 80,000 kinds of plants.

_____ 2. "New" plants can provide food energy and protein.

_____ 3. It is difficult for people to start eating different food, but it is possible.

_____ 4. Soybeans are rich in protein.

_____ 5. People all over the world have learned to enjoy eating peanuts.

WORD STUDY

I. PREPOSITIONS

You have learned a few common meanings and uses of prepositions. There are often no rules or direct translations at all. You must just learn them by practicing.

Put the right prepositions in these sentences.

1. Millions _____ people are building houses _____ land that used to be farms.
2. There are 350,000 kinds _____ plants _____ the world.
3. _____ these, 80,000 are suitable food _____ humans.
4. It is common _____ developing countries _____ people _____ depend _____ only one or two plants _____ their food.
5. Corn, wheat, and rice are _____ 8 percent and 14 percent protein.
6. Soybeans are an important food _____ China and Japan.
7. There are other plants that are rich _____ protein.
8. People _____ parts _____ Southeast Asia eat winged beans.
9. Food is a very important part _____ our lives, and it is often difficult to change _____ a different kind _____ food.

II. CONTEXT CLUES

Many words have more than one meaning. Choose the meaning for each word as it is used in the sentence.

1. You are too late to see the volleyball game. It is <u>all</u> <u>over</u>. It was a very fast game, and our team won.
   a. finished
   b. everywhere
   c. above
   d. 100 percent
2. The children were very <u>still</u> as they watched TV. No one made any noise.
   a. yet
   b. quite
   c. quiet
   d. even
3. After you put the letter in the envelope, <u>seal</u> the envelope so the letter cannot fall out.
   a. an animal that lives in the sea
   b. fasten something together
   c. sell
   d. write the address
4. I could see the <u>figure</u> of a man. I couldn't tell who it was because he was too far away.
   a. shape
   b. number
   c. guess
   d. photograph
5. In a supermarket, apples and tomatoes are in the <u>produce</u>[3] department.
   a. farming
   b. make or grow
   c. fruit and vegetable
   d. crops

[3] Pronunciation: pró-duce.

6. The captain of the ship <u>ordered</u> his men to get ready to enter port.
   a. put in the right way
   b. asked for food in a restaurant
   c. told someone to do something
   d. put the smallest numbers first

AMNESTY INTERNATIONAL

Right now, somewhere in the world, someone is writing a letter. The letter is addressed to a president or king, a general, or the head of the police in another country. The letter is about someone the writer does not even
5 know. The writer is an ordinary person who has never met a king or a general.

The writer is one of the 200,000 members of Amnesty International. This organization was started in 1961 to help people who are put in prison only because of their
10 race, their religion, or their beliefs. They neither used violence nor suggested that others use it. There are over half a million of these prisoners.

In the main Amnesty International office in London, people gather information about prisoners in over one
15 hundred countries. They send this information to Amnesty groups in more than forty countries. Each group receives information on two prisoners from countries of different political systems. Then the members start writing letters.

A government that holds prisoners receives hundreds
20 of letters. Each letter asks very politely that the prisoners be freed. The government knows that the prisoners are not forgotten. The world cares about them.

Amnesty International works in other ways. It writes reports on governments and prisons. These reports are
25 printed in newspapers. Sometimes it sends a famous lawyer to attend a trial or to talk with important people in the government. It helps the families of prisoners. The pressure never stops. <u>So far</u>, thousands of prisoners have   (until now)
been freed because of the work of Amnesty International.
30 Hundreds of others have received better food, visits from their families, or medical care.

Why do people take the time to write letters to help strangers? Members of Amnesty International know that their letters can be successful. They know this is a way
35 to take direct action to help other human beings.

The world knows this too. In 1977, Amnesty International received the Nobel Peace Prize, one of the most important international prizes that any person or organization can win. It won the prize because thousands of
40 ordinary people care enough about human rights to write letters. The Amnesty International candle, a sign of light and hope, shines all over the world.

I. VOCABULARY

trial	medical	politely	organization
so far	beliefs	violence	general
suggested	received	lawyer	candle
printed	pressure	prize	religion
members	reports		

1. The _____ called Amnesty International was started in 1961.
2. It helps people who are put in prison only because of their race, their _____, or their _____.
3. The prisoners neither used _____ nor _____ that others use it.
4. Each letter asks very _____ that the prisoners be freed.
5. Amnesty International writes reports that are _____ in newspapers.
6. Sometimes it sends a famous _____ to attend a _____.
7. The _____ never stops.
8. _____, thousands of prisoners have been freed because of the work of Amnesty International.
9. Hundreds of prisoners have received better food or _____ care.
10. _____ know that their letters can be successful.
11. In 1977, Amnesty International received the Nobel Peace _____.
12. The Amnesty International _____, a sign of light and hope, shines all over the world.

II. VOCABULARY (new context)

pressure	prize	violence	suggested
medical	trial	organization	candle
print	polite	lawyer	so far
general	members	religions	beliefs

1. Farming magazines sometimes _____ information about new plants.
2. The man who killed his wife will have his _____ next week. He has a good lawyer.
3. It is _____ to shake hands when you are introduced to someone.
4. Most North American universities have an _____ of foreign students. They help new students, plan trips and parties, and do other things together.
5. Hospitals, doctors, and nurses provide _____ care.
6. A _____ provides less light than an electric light.
7. Luis won a _____ for writing the best engineering paper.

8. Christianity and Islam are important world _____.
9. A person must attend four years of a university and three years of law school to become a _____.
10. People who are overweight often have high blood _____.
11. The teacher _____ several interesting places for the students to visit.
12. _____, they have been too busy to go anywhere.
13. All the _____ of David's family went to a university.
14. There is a lot of _____ in New York. People fight and kill each other.
15. A religion is a system of _____.

III. VOCABULARY REVIEW: Opposites

Match each word with its opposite.

1. similar	a. solution
2. common	b. send
3. prevent	c. unusual
4. problem	d. not probable
5. improve	e. finished
6. peace	f. get better
7. likely	g. cause
8. safe	h. get worse
9. incomplete	i. general
10. receive	j. dangerous
	k. different
	l. war

IV. ORAL QUESTIONS

1. To whom do Amnesty International members write?
2. What kind of prisoners do they write about?
3. Did these prisoners use violence?
4. Where is the main Amnesty International office?
5. Amnesty International writes letters. What else does it do?

6. How has the work of Amnesty International helped prisoners so far?
7. Why do people take the time to write letters to strangers?
8. What prize did Amnesty International receive?

V. COMPREHENSION

1. Amnesty International letters are written by _____.
   a. kings and generals
   b. ordinary people
   c. lawyers and police
   d. important people in the government
2. Amnesty International helps people _____.
   a. who are in prison for their beliefs or race
   b. who used violence against the government
   c. in over forty countries
   d. who do not have electricity
3. Each member writes _____.
   a. hundreds of letters per month
   b. reports that are printed in newspapers
   c. letters about two or three prisoners per month
   d. to famous lawyers to get help for prisoners
4. Members get their information from _____ so they can write letters.
   a. prisoners
   b. the office in London
   c. presidents and generals
   d. famous lawyers
5. Amnesty International won the Nobel Prize for _____.
   a. history
   b. chemistry
   c. mathematics
   d. peace
*6. Which of these is probably NOT true?
   a. Amnesty International is organized very well.
   b. Anyone can become a member of Amnesty International.
   c. A president of a country likes getting letters from all over the world about a prisoner.
   d. Amnesty International members write letters to all kinds of governments.

VI. MAIN IDEA

Choose the three main ideas.
Amnesty International _____.

_____ 1. helps prisoners who use violence.
_____ 2. helps people who are in prison because of their beliefs, religion, or race.
_____ 3. writes letters, writes reports, and sends lawyers to help prisoners.
_____ 4. writes letters to kings.
_____ 5. is successful because it has helped thousands of prisoners.
_____ 6. uses a candle as a sign of light and hope.

WORD STUDY

I. WORD FORMS

Some common adjective endings are -al, -able, -ful, -less, -t, and -ous. Write the correct form of each word in the blank.

Verb	Noun	Adjective
1. experiment	experiment	experimental
2.	nature	natural
3. prevent	prevention	preventable
4. suit		suitable
5. believe	belief	(un)believable
6. succeed	success	(un)successful
7.	violence	violent
8. differ	difference	different
9.	religion	religious
10. use	use	useful, useless

1. Scientists are _____ with plants that produce oil.
2. Arizona Indians used to live close to _____. Some of them still do.
3. Many common diseases of the nineteenth century are _____ now.
4. Yellow does not _____ you very well. You look better in blue.

5. That story is _____. It can't be true.
6. The first experiment with the new crop did not _____. The plants died.
7. Mr. Dunn was so angry that he became _____. We had to call the police.
8. Plants _____ greatly in the amount of protein they contain.
9. Helen is very _____. She goes to church every day.
10. The jojoba is likely to become a _____ plant.

II. WORD FORMS: Adjectives

Adjectives have only one form. There is no plural. Be careful with this kind of adjective:

> She has a <u>two-week</u> vacation.
> It is a <u>two-hour</u> drive from Ottawa to Montreal.

Don't use a plural form.
Use a hyphen (-).

Use the information in parentheses to fill in the blanks.

1. It is a _____ flight from Los Angeles to London. (ten hours)
2. High school students in California have a _____ vacation in the summer. (three months)
3. It is a _____ drive from Toronto to Winnipeg. (four days)
4. It is a _____ trip from New York to Boston. (200 kilometers)
5. Mary won the _____ race. (1,000 meters)

III. CONTEXT CLUES

1. Farmers get more crops per hectare by using modern farming <u>methods</u>. They use better seeds and different ways to make the land rich. They do most of the work with machines.
   a. machines
   c. animals
   b. better seeds
   d. ways of doing something
2. If you want to have a garden, first choose a place with good <u>soil</u>. Plant

the seeds in the <u>soil</u>. Water them, and in a few days you will see small plants growing.

    a. land or dirt   c. water and sun

    b. seeds or plants   d. petroleum

3. Parents <u>protect</u> their children from danger. They take care of their children all the time when they are small. They teach them to be careful of cars and of fire.

    a. provide   c. give an education

    b. keep away from danger   d. develop

4. <u>Even though</u> I had a big dinner two hours ago, I feel a little hungry. I guess I'll have some coffee and cake.

    a. nevertheless   c. although

    b. and   d. however

5. The USSR is a <u>huge</u> country. It is the biggest in the world in area.

    a. large population   c. in the North

    b. very large   d. new

Old Faithful Geyser, Yellowstone National Park
National Park Service Photograph

Yellowstone River Canyon, Upper Falls
National Park Service Photograph

NATIONAL PARKS

Canada and the United States are huge countries that stretch from the Atlantic Ocean to the Pacific Ocean. For centuries the North American Indians lived close to nature, using only what they needed. But when the Europeans
5 arrived, they saw an endless supply of materials they could use and sell. They killed the animals and cut the forests. They used farming methods that allowed the wind and rain to take away the rich topsoil. They did not worry because there were always more forests, animals, and
10 farmlands.

Nevertheless, a few people thought about the future. They traveled and saw the magnificent scenery in the West—the snow-covered mountains, clear lakes, and huge trees. They worried that their grandchildren would
15 never see these natural wonders. Instead they would see farms and cities where there had once been wild beauty.

This handful of people persuaded their governments to start national park systems. The parks would protect
20 places of great beauty, of scientific interest, or with unusual plants and animals. The two governments would take care of them and keep them natural forever.

In 1872 the United States government passed a law making Yellowstone National Park, in Wyoming, the
25 first park to belong to all the people in the country. It is an area with geysers, <u>hot springs</u>, waterfalls, and lakes.

A few years later Canada named Banff, in Alberta, its first national park. It protects magnificent lakes, mountains, and forests.

30 Both countries continued to add parks to the systems.

Later parks included not only natural beauty but the remains of Indian societies. Others protect areas that were important in the exploration and history of the two countries.

35   Most of the population of Canada have always lived along the southern border, and the rest of the country was mostly empty and wild. But after World War II, development increased much faster. <u>Even though</u> the North   (although) did not develop as fast as the South, more and more
40 people realized it was important to save the large populations of <u>wildlife</u> before it was too late.   (wild animals)

   Today national parks protect scenic and historical areas from Hawaii to Newfoundland. The parks cover millions of hectares in the mountains, the deserts, the forests, and
45 along the coasts. There are museums, hotels, and restaurants for visitors. Scientists, naturalists, and historians show films and give talks.

   Other countries have developed national park systems, too. People everywhere in the world can enjoy the natural
50 beauty of their countries and know it is protected. And they know the parks will be there for the enjoyment of their children and their children's children.

I. VOCABULARY

even though	huge	methods	protect
persuaded	materials	scenery	forever
topsoil	magnificent	waterfalls	border
worry	naturalist	remains	wildlife

1. Canada and the United States are _____ countries.
2. Europeans saw an endless supply of _____ they could use and sell.
3. They used farming _____ that allowed the wind and rain to take away the rich _____.
4. Some people traveled and saw the magnificent _____ in the West.
5. This handful of people _____ their two governments to start national park systems.

6. The parks would _____ places of great beauty and scientific interest.
7. The two governments would keep the parks natural _____.
8. Yellowstone is an area of geysers, hot springs, _____, and lakes.
9. Banff protects _____ lakes, mountains, and forests.
10. Later parks included the _____ of Indian societies.
11. Most of the population of Canada has always lived along the southern _____.
12. _____ the North did not develop as fast as the South, more and more people realized it was important to save the large populations of _____.

II. VOCABULARY (new context)

persuaded	huge	protect	waterfall
remains	print	method	scenery
forever	materials	border	even though
soil	instead of		

1. When Helen and David got married, they promised to love each other _____.
2. The whale is a _____ animal that lives in the sea.
3. Niagara Falls is a famous _____ on the border between Canada and the United States.
4. When you cross the _____ of a country, you usually have to show your passport.
5. Traditional village houses in Syria and Malaya are made from different _____.
6. Tourists can see the _____ of Greek and Roman cities around the Mediterranean Sea.
7. Fast-food restaurants all use the same _____ to cook hamburgers. They cook them in the same way.
8. Carol _____ her parents that she was old enough to travel to Chicago alone. They allowed her to go.
9. People in desert areas need to _____ themselves from the sun.
10. Switzerland has magnificent _____. The mountains and lakes are beautiful.

11. I think I'll go swimming _____ it's not very hot today.
12. Jojoba and buffalo gourds will grow in poor _____.

III. VOCABULARY REVIEW

unfortunately	canals	whether	condition
frightening	bushes	figure	wheat
out	level	up	increase
needles	bear		

1. It would be _____ to meet Dracula on a dark night.
2. If you use _____ all the rice, I'll buy some more at the super-market.
3. Mr. and Mrs. Banker planted three trees and several _____ in front of their new house.
4. The Jensens own a large _____ farm in Alberta.
5. Please ask her _____ she is going home or to the shopping center.
6. George bought a cheap car, but _____ it needs a lot of work. It is in very poor _____.
7. There is an _____ in corn production this year. Farmers have grown more corn than last year.
8. In California a system of _____ brings water to the farms.
9. This table is not _____. One leg is shorter than the others.
10. Evergreen trees have _____ instead of leaves. These trees are used for Christmas trees.

IV. ORAL QUESTIONS

1. How did the Europeans destroy forests and farmlands in North America?
2. Why did some people want to start a national park system?
3. What kinds of places do national parks protect? Name five.
4. Where was the first national park?
*5. Why do most of the population of Canada live along the southern border?

6. What services and programs do national parks offer?

*7. There has been a large increase in visitors to national parks during the last twenty years. What problems does this cause?

*8. What do naturalists talk about in national parks programs?

V. COMPREHENSION

1. For centuries North American Indians _____.
   a. lived near the Canadian border
   b. lived close to nature
   c. lived in national parks
   d. visited museums in national parks

2. Europeans thought the supply of materials in North America was _____.
   a. used up
   b. overcrowded
   c. dangerous
   d. endless

3. A handful of people wanted national parks to protect _____ for their grandchildren.
   a. farmlands
   b. places of great beauty
   c. rich topsoil
   d. museums

*4. Wyoming is a _____.
   a. village
   b. city
   c. state
   d. country

5. Later parks protected areas _____.
   a. important in human history
   b. with geysers and hot springs
   c. near the border
   d. destroyed by poor farming methods

*6. The northern part of Canada has probably developed slowly because of _____.
   a. the desert
   b. the Indians
   c. the climate
   d. the wildlife

*7. Which one is probably NOT true?
   a. Many countries of the world have national parks.
   b. You can learn a lot at a national park.
   c. There are no wild places left in North America for new national parks.
   d. The national park system in the United States had its 100th birthday in 1972.

VI. MAIN IDEA

Choose the one main idea.

_____ 1. The national park system protects beautiful and historic places for present and future enjoyment.
_____ 2. Poor farming methods destroy the topsoil.
_____ 3. There are beautiful mountains in Banff National Park.
_____ 4. National parks protect wildlife so our grandchildren can see wild animals.

WORD STUDY

I. WORD FORMS

Use the correct form.

Verb	Noun	Adjective
1.	scene scenery	scenic
2.	science scientist	scientific
3. persuade	persuasion	persuasive
4. protect	protection	protective
5. continue	continuation	continuous
6.	history historian	historical
7. enjoy	enjoyment	(un)enjoyable
8. suggest	suggestion	
9. organize	organization	
10. solve	solution	

1. This picture is a _____ in Newfoundland.
2. Chemistry is one kind of _____.
3. He is a very _____ person. He could persuade you to do almost anything.
4. Some of the huge redwood trees in California are under the _____ of the National Park Service.

5. Workers get very tired from the _____ noise in a factory.
6. Most countries have a _____ museum.
7. A visit to a national park is _____ for the whole family.
8. I would like to make a _____ for your trip. A train ride across Canada is beautiful.
9. The United Nations has _____ an international conference on the sea.
10. They are trying to _____ the problem of coastal fishing rights.

II. PREPOSITIONS

Write the correct preposition in each blank.

1. Canada and the United States stretch _____ the Atlantic Ocean _____ the Pacific Ocean.
2. For centuries the North American Indians lived close _____ nature.
3. The Europeans saw an endless supply _____ materials they could use and sell.
4. Nevertheless, a few people thought _____ the future.
5. They saw the magnificent scenery _____ the West.
6. The parks would protect places _____ great beauty, _____ scientific interest, or _____ unusual plants and animals.
7. In 1872 the United States passed a law making Yellowstone National Park, _____ Wyoming, the first park to belong _____ all the people _____ the country.
8. Both countries continued _____ add parks _____ the systems.
9. Most _____ the population _____ Canada has always lived _____ the southern border.
10. The parks cover millions _____ hectares _____ the mountains and _____ the coasts.

III. CONTEXT CLUES

1. There is a <u>pond</u> near the Whites' home. The children go fishing and swimming there.
   a. small lake
   b. barrel
   c. plant
   d. swimming pool

2. This bathroom is so small that if you <u>spread</u> your arms, you can touch both walls.
   a. move
   b. lift over your head
   c. stretch
   d. turn to the left

3. Abdullah was a student here last year. However, he is <u>no longer</u> here because he went home to Libya.
   a. shorter
   b. not anymore
   c. not the longest
   d. so far

4. When you <u>multiply</u> 5 by 4, the answer is 20.
   a. +
   b. −
   c. ×
   d. ÷

5. Last winter there was a lot of snow in the mountains. Then there were heavy rains in the spring. The Mississippi River rose so high that it <u>flooded</u> thousands of hectares. The land was too wet to plant crops, and fifty houses were destroyed.
   a. planted
   b. watered
   c. moved
   d. covered with water

THE BEAVER

The beaver lives in the forests of the United States and
Canada. It spends its time cutting down trees to build and
<u>repair</u> its houses and dams. Although it is a hardworking   (mend, fix)
animal, it sometimes takes time to play in the water.

5 It seems impossible, but this animal was very important
in history. It was the cause of 150 years of fighting among
the Dutch, the French, and the English. It was the main
reason for the French and Indian War. This war, which
the English fought against the French and Indians, de-
10 stroyed the government of the Iroquois[1] Indians. These
Indians lived in the northeastern United States and parts
of Canada. The beaver was also one of the reasons that
men explored the waterways stretching across the two
countries.

15 The beaver spends most of its time in the water, so it
always builds its house near a stream. The house is made
of pieces of wood, rocks, plants, and mud (dirt mixed

---

[1] Pronunciation: eár-uh-quoy.

with water). It is very safe because the only entrance is
through a tunnel under the water. The only opening
20 above the water is a small airhole.

     The beaver also builds a dam to make a <u>pond</u> near the   (small lake)
house. It uses sticks, mud, rocks, and plants to build a
dam across the stream. This makes a pond that is about a
meter deep and can cover four hectares.

25   No one teaches the beaver how to build houses and
dams. It is born knowing how to do this. It has two large,
sharp front teeth for cutting down trees. These teeth
never stop growing. It can use its front feet like hands. Its
back feet spread out until they are twenty centimeters
30 wide for swimming. When the beaver swims, it steers with
its flat tail. It can also use its tail to warn the other beavers
of danger. It hits the water with its tail to make a loud
noise. From its head to the end of its tail, it is about a
meter long.

35   The beaver moves very slowly on land, but it is an ex-

cellent swimmer. Although it is a mammal, it can stay underwater for fifteen minutes and can swim almost a kilometer without coming up for air.

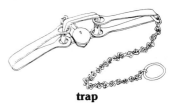
trap

40 In the eighteenth century, men started trapping the beaver and selling its skins in Europe and North America. Beaver hats became very popular, and the skins were used for other clothes. Men walked and traveled in small boats from the Atlantic to the Pacific, trapping beaver and exploring new land. Beaver skins, called brown gold,

45 were very important in North American <u>commerce</u>, and (buying and selling) they were often used instead of money. The Dutch, French, and English colonies fought over the best trapping areas.

In the eighteenth century, there were millions of bea-
50 vers. By 1900 they were almost all gone. Men had over-trapped them, and there were cities and farms where they used to live.

beaver hat

Then both the Canadian and United States govern-ments passed laws to protect beavers. However, the bea-
55 ver had few natural enemies left, and now humans were no longer an enemy. Each mother bears four or five ba-bies a year, and the beaver population began to <u>multiply</u>.   (2 × 3 = 6)

Naturalists say some areas are overpopulated with beavers. They cut down young forests and fruit trees.
60 Their dams flood land and cause serious damage. Both governments now allow some trapping, but no one knows whether this will solve the problem or not. Perhaps beaver hats will have to become popular again in order to control the beaver population.

I. VOCABULARY

mud	damage	commerce	flood
skins	spread	dam	no longer
repair	multiply	steers	sharp
warn	stream	pond	trapping

1. The beaver spends its time cutting down trees to build and _____ its houses and dams.
2. It always builds its house near a _____.

3. The house is made of pieces of wood, rocks, and _____ (dirt mixed with water).
4. The beaver also builds a _____ to make a _____.
5. It has two large, _____ front teeth for cutting down trees.
6. Its back feet _____ out until they are twenty centimeters wide for swimming.
7. When it swims, it _____ with its broad, flat tail.
8. It can also use its tail to _____ the other beavers of danger.
9. In the eighteenth century, men started _____ beavers.
10. Beaver skins were very important in _____.
11. Humans were _____ an enemy.
12. The beaver population began to _____.
13. Their dams _____ land.
14. This causes serious _____.

II. VOCABULARY (new context)

pond	commerce	dam	sharp
repair	even though	no longer	spread
flooded	damage	mud	warned
stream	steering	trapping	multiply

1. The Aswan _____ on the Nile River made a lake that is 500 kilometers long.
2. My car broke down, but I can _____ it myself.
3. This knife won't cut anything. It isn't _____ enough.
4. When you drive a car, never take both hands off the _____ wheel.
5. One of the children left the water running in the shower and _____ the bathroom floor.
6. Most Hawaiians _____ speak Hawaiian. They speak English now.
7. Ms. Baker _____ her children to be careful in the swimming pool.
8. The fire in their garage caused $5,000 worth of _____.
9. When it rains, a dirt road becomes covered with _____.
10. John took a piece of bread and _____ butter on it.
11. Water in a _____ is continuously moving to a new place.
12. A _____ is like a mirror when the water is still.
13. _____ animals is not allowed in national parks.
14. England has a long history of _____ with other countries.

III. VOCABULARY REVIEW

violence	trial	border	soil
lawyer	candle	prize	scenery
whether	printed	handle	pain

1. There is an important _____ for a man who stole money from the government.
2. He has a famous _____.
3. He did not use _____ to steal the money.
4. The _____ in Hawaii is beautiful.
5. There is a _____ for the best student.
6. The name of the prizewinner will be _____ in the newspaper.
7. Plants need sun, water, and good _____.
8. People cannot _____ the things in museums.

IV. ORAL QUESTIONS

1. Describe a beaver.
2. Describe a beaver's house.
3. How does the beaver know how to build houses and dams?
4. Why did trappers kill so many beavers in the eighteenth century?
5. How did the beaver destroy a government?
6. How do beavers cause damage today?
*7. Where is a beaver safer from an enemy, on the land or in the water? Why?

V. COMPREHENSION: True/False

_____ 1. The beaver learns how to make dams from its parents.
_____ 2. Naturalists explored waterways in the eighteenth century to study beavers.
_____ *3. The beaver uses similar materials and methods to build dams and houses.
_____ 4. The beaver builds its house near a stream.
_____ 5. A beaver steers with its front feet when it swims.
_____ *6. Beaver hats are popular in North America today but not in Europe.
_____ 7. Trappers killed too many beavers.
_____ *8. A beaver can breathe underwater.

VI. MAIN IDEA: Supporting Details

Read the three main ideas listed below. Write the letter of each supporting detail under the correct main idea.

1. The beaver's body   2. What the beaver does   3. Beavers and humans

a. It has a broad flat tail.
b. It uses its tail to warn other beavers of danger.
c. It is about a meter long.
d. Beaver hats became very popular in the eighteenth century.
e. It builds a house with an underwater entrance.
f. By 1900 the beavers were almost all gone.
g. The beaver's teeth never stop growing.
h. Beaver skins were called brown gold.

WORD STUDY

I. SUFFIXES: -ize Verbs

You can change some words into verbs by adding -ize. The verb means to make into, to cause to be.

Example: Radio helped popularize country music. (Radio helped make country music popular.)

Add -ize to each word. Then put the right verb in each sentence. Use the correct tense.

Spelling: Drop the final y.

memory	colony	modern
winter	special	industrial

1. Spain and Portugal _____ Latin America.
2. The Greens bought a beautiful old house. They _____ the kitchen. They did not change the rest of the house.

3. Dolores wants to _____ in developing better kinds of corn.
4. Please _____ the new vocabulary. There is a test tomorrow.
5. Developing countries want to _____ as fast as possible. They are building modern factories.
6. The Davis family has a small summer house in the mountains. They are going to _____ it and put in a big fireplace. Then they can stay there to go skiing in the winter.

II. NOUN SUBSTITUTES

Look at these words in the reading selection. Then tell what each work means.

1.	page 131	line	3	its	6.	page 132	line 26	this
2.		line	8	which	7.		line 26	it
3.		line	15	it	8.	page 133	line 46	they
4.	page 132	line	18	it	9.		line 51	they
5.		line	23	this	10.		line 59	they

III. WORD FORMS

Put the right form in each sentence.

	Verb	Noun	Adjective
1.		mud	muddy
2.	sharpen		sharp
3.	live	life, plural = lives	
4.	trap	trap	
		trapper	
5.		commerce	commercial
6.	multiply	multiplication	
7.	save	safety	safe, safety
8.	destroy	destruction	destructive
9.	enter	entrance	
10.	sell	sale	

1. It is raining, and the floor is _____ where the children walked on it.
2. May I please _____ my pencil?

3. A cat has nine _____.
4. A rabbit was caught in the beaver _____.
5. There are a lot of _____ on TV. They try to persuade you to buy something.
6. _____ is easier than division.
7. There is a list of _____ rules by the swimming pool at our apartment building.
8. Floods cause millions of dollars worth of _____ every year.
9. Please _____ the building through the front entrance.
10. This old house is for _____, but no one wants to buy it. It would cost too much to modernize it.

IV. CONTEXT CLUES

1. If you throw a heavy rock in the water, it will go down to the bottom. If you throw in a light piece of wood, it will <u>float</u>.
   - a. go to the bottom of water
   - b. ride on the top of water
   - c. fly
   - d. get wet
2. The cold Peru <u>Current</u> moves from Antarctica north along the west coast of South America. This cold water changes the climate in Chile and Peru.
   - a. a river in the ocean
   - b. lately
   - c. a large ship
   - d. a whale
3. My homework is <u>entirely</u> finished. I did it all.
   - a. go in
   - b. mostly
   - c. partly
   - d. completely
4. Joan is going to have a party tonight, so she has to <u>prepare</u> for it. She has to clean her apartment, go to the supermarket, and cook some food.
   - a. cook
   - b. play music
   - c. get ready
   - d. buy some cassettes
5. What is the <u>value</u> of this gold necklace? It is worth $500.
   - a. color
   - b. worth
   - c. valley
   - d. size
6. John was a <u>tiny</u> baby when he was born. He weighed only two kilos.
   - a. very small
   - b. very large
   - c. huge
   - d. thin

ANTARCTICA

Center for Polar and Scientific Archives, Washington, D.C.

Antarctica is cold. Everything is white. Only a few black rocks and green plants in iceless valleys add some color to the endless white cover of ice. It is a land of wild magnificence.

5   The ice in Antarctica is thousands of meters deep and formed at least 20,000 years ago. It contains 85 percent

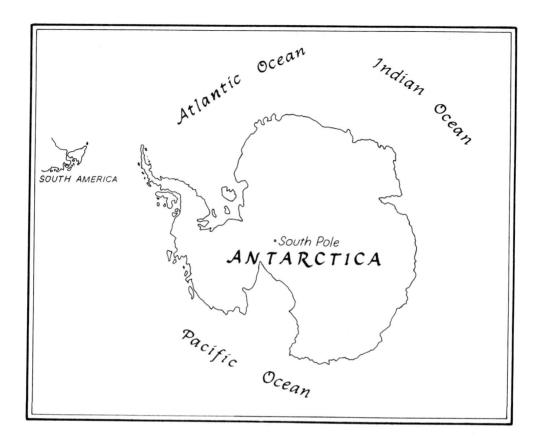

of all the fresh water on the earth. At the edges, <u>icebergs</u>
break off and float on the ocean currents to warmer climates. An iceberg can cover four square kilometers. In
10 winter storms, winds blow up to 400 kilometers an hour.

(completely)

This land of unimaginable cold must be <u>entirely</u> dead.
Surely nothing could live here.

But even in this impossible climate, there is life. The icy
cold water of the Antarctic Ocean contains <u>tiny</u> plants.

(very small)

15 For two months every summer they receive sunlight almost twenty-four hours a day. At this time the Antarctic
is probably the most productive ocean in the world. These
plants provide food for millions of <u>krill</u>, an animal that is
less than eight centimeters long. The krill provides food
20 for seabirds, fish, seals, whales, and penguins. Some of
these animals provide food for humans.

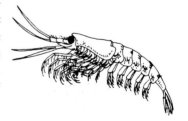

Since 1960 something unusual has been happening in Antarctica. Scientists from many countries have been working together in this huge laboratory. Even though a
25 few countries have divided Antarctica among themselves, it is the first part of the world used entirely for peaceful purposes.

These scientists are interested in several things. They know that this huge icy area is very important to the
30 world's climate, but they are trying to learn why. They think there is petroleum under the ice, but they have not discovered any yet. The world needs protein, and a dozen countries are experimenting on how to catch and prepare krill for commercial use. Several kinds of fish may have
35 commercial <u>value</u> also.

penguin

(worth)

It is difficult to know what will happen in Antarctica. Companies may discover petroleum and dig oil wells. But winds or icebergs could knock over the equipment and cause serious damage to the area. There are rich
40 fishing areas, but in the 1970s the USSR overfished Antarctic codfish. Hundreds of thousands of whales used to live in the icy waters. Now there are only a few thousand left. Krill is very important in the Antarctic chain of life. Other animals depend on it for food. However, no one
45 knows how much could be safely caught for human use without breaking the chain of life.

Some people are very encouraged because different countries are working together peacefully in Antarctica. They suggest that these countries should internationalize
50 Antarctica. Just as national parks belong to all the people in a country, Antarctica could belong to all the people in the world.

I. VOCABULARY

penguins	float	knock	icebergs
currents	encouraged	entirely	internationalize
commercial	value	chain	prepare
tiny	krill		

1. At the edges of Antarctica _____ break off.
2. They _____ on the ocean _____ to warmer climates.
3. This land of unimaginable cold must be _____ dead.
4. The icy cold water of the Antarctic Ocean contains _____ plants.
5. These plants provide food for millions of _____.
6. The krill provides food for fish, seals, whales, and _____.
7. A dozen countries are experimenting on how to catch and _____ krill.
8. Several kinds of fish may have commercial _____ also.
9. Winds could _____ over the oil well equipment.
10. Krill is very important in the Antarctic _____ of life.
11. Some people are very _____ because different countries are working together peacefully in Antarctica.

II. VOCABULARY (new context)

tiny	value	float	commerce
current	icebergs	penguins	prepare
entirely	knocked	sharp	chain
encourage			

1. Old houses were made _____ of natural materials. No plastic was used.
2. A boat can _____ downstream on a river, but it needs some kind of power to go upstream.
3. Hiroko has to give a report tomorrow on her visit to a national park. She has to _____ her talk tonight.
4. In July there are thousands of _____ in the North Atlantic. They break off the ice in Greenland and float south.
5. Norway is warmer than you would guess because the warm Norwegian _____ moves north along the coast.
6. _____ look as if they were dressed for dinner at an expensive hotel.
7. People in developing countries put a high _____ on education. They think it is very important.
8. Teachers _____ beginning English students to talk even though they make mistakes.

9. The only jewelry she wore was a thin gold _____ around her neck.
10. Mary _____ over her Eskimo carving, but it just rolled around on the table. It did not break.
11. Huge trees grow from _____ seeds.

III. VOCABULARY REVIEW

Underline one word that does not belong with the others.

1. wind, rain, whether, storms
2. law, trial, lawyer, engineer
3. persuade, trap, hunt, fish
4. stream, pond, waterfall, river
5. violence, fighting, solution, war
6. rice, corn, beans, wheat
7. add, multiply, divide, repair
8. steer, hurt, damage, destroy

IV. ORAL QUESTIONS

1. Describe what Antarctica looks like.
2. Why is the Antarctic Ocean so productive in summer?
3. How is the krill important in the chain of life?
*4. In what months do scientists go to Antarctica?
5. What are scientists studying in Antarctica?
*6. What might happen if fishing companies kill too many krill?
*7. What might happen if an iceberg hit the equipment at an oil well in the Peru Current?
*8. Why do some people want to internationalize Antarctica?

V. COMPREHENSION: True/False

_____ 1. Most of Antarctica is covered with ice.
_____ 2. This area is entirely dead because it is so cold.
_____ 3. Antarctica contains 85 percent of all the salt water in the world.
_____ 4. Tiny plants grow in the Antarctic Ocean.
_____ *5. The Antarctic Ocean is the most productive in July and August.

_____ 6. Krill is rich in protein.

_____ *7. Oil companies probably want to internationalize Antarctica.

VI. MAIN IDEA

Choose the three main ideas.

_____ 1. Antarctica and the Antarctic Ocean are very cold, but plants and animals live there.

_____ 2. Antarctica contains 85 percent of all the fresh water on earth and has winds up to 400 kilometers per hour.

_____ 3. National parks belong to all the people in a country.

_____ 4. Scientists from many countries are working together peacefully in Antarctica.

_____ 5. Commercial development in Antarctica is possible, but it could cause problems.

WORD STUDY

I. SUFFIXES: -ive

The adjective form -ive means able to do something.

> Example: David is very persuasive. He can persuade anyone to do anything.

Choose the correct adjective for each sentence.

	Adjective
product	(un)productive
imagine	(un)imaginative
act	(in)active
destruction	(non)destructive
protect	(un)protective

1. Osamu is very _____ in the International Students Organization.
2. Desert soil is _____ without water.
3. Some children are very _____. They break all their toys.
4. Ms. Miller is very _____ of her children. She is almost too careful.
5. Most TV programs are not very _____. You can guess what will happen.

II. WORD FORMS

Verb	Noun	Adjective
1. prepare	preparation	
2. value	value	valuable
3. encourage	encouragement	encouraging
4.	ice	icy
5. imagine	imagination	(un)imaginable
6. produce	product	(un)productive
	production	
7. discover	discovery	
8. depend	(in)dependence	(in)dependent
		(un)dependable
9. educate	education	educational
10. colonize	colony	colonial

Choose the correct word for each blank.

1. Careful _____ is necessary for a successful experiment.
2. Gold is more _____ than silver.
3. George succeeded at the university because his parents gave him so much _____.
4. There were several accidents last night because of the _____ streets.
5. Use your _____. Describe what life will be like in a hundred years.
6. Japan has greatly increased its _____ of cars.
7. Marie Curie made an important scientific _____.
8. David is very _____. If he says he will do something, you know he will do it.

9. Films used in the classroom are _____. Films at movie theaters are for enjoyment.

10. People in Quebec speak French because Quebec was a French _____.

III. CONTEXT CLUES

1. Bill was sitting in his room doing his homework. Suddenly the wind blew the door shut, and a picture fell off the wall and broke. When his mother came into the room, Bill explained, "It's not my fault. The wind made the picture fall."
   a. It didn't happen because of me.
   b. It's not my picture.
   c. The wind was blowing.
   d. I did it.

2. Z is the final letter in the alphabet.
   a. first
   b. most important
   c. least important
   d. last

3. Some plants are poisonous. If you eat them, you will die.
   a. rich in protein
   b. can kill you
   c. can provide energy
   d. beautiful

4. People felt great sorrow when President Kennedy was killed.
   a. sadness
   b. energy
   c. damage
   d. smoothness

5. When you cry, tears come out of your eyes.
   a. pieces of dirt
   b. breaks paper into pieces
   c. dust
   d. drops of water

CRYING

Mary sells houses for a large company. A couple has agreed to buy a house for $150,000. They are going to come into the office this afternoon to sign the final papers. Then her boss calls her into his office. The buyers have

5 changed their minds. The boss is very angry and speaks
  <u>rudely</u> to Mary. She knows it is not her fault, but he will   (not politely)
  not listen. She also knows she will lose a lot of money,
  and she was planning to buy a new car. She bursts into
  tears.
10   Paul is sitting in the backyard with his wife and children.
  They have just finished dinner and are having a pleasant
  evening talking. The phone rings. It is Paul's mother calling from another city. Paul's father has just had a heart
  attack and died. Paul starts crying as he tells his mother
15 he will come as soon as possible.
      In Atlantic City the Miss America competition is nearly
  finished. There are ten finalists. The judges choose Miss
  Alabama as the most beautiful woman in the United
  States. When her name is announced, she steps forward.
20 The outgoing Miss America places a crown on her head,
  and the new Miss America starts to cry.
      People cry when they feel very bad. They cry when
  something terrible happens, like a death in the family.
  They cry in sorrow when a close friend has a death in
25 the family. They cry when they feel very sad or very
  angry. They cry when they know they cannot do anything about a problem, and they feel helpless.
      People also cry when they feel very good. They cry
  when they have been very worried about something but
30 find out everything is all right. They cry when something
  wonderful happens.
      How do people feel about crying? Paul felt better after
  he let out his feelings. Miss America was so excited she
  hardly knew she was crying. Mary was embarrassed and
35 very angry with herself because she cried in her boss's
  office.
      In the United States until lately, men were not sup-
  posed to cry. Crying was weak and only for women.
  Men were supposed to be strong. But things are changing.
40 Men are beginning to realize that it is all right to show
  their feelings. Women are learning that sometimes they
  can do something about a problem instead of just crying.
  They try not to cry in a public place or in front of a
  frightened child.

45   Chemists have been studying why people cry. They say the body produces two kinds of tears. One kind cleans out the eye if it gets dirt in it. But when people cry because of their feelings, these tears have poison chemicals in them. The body is getting rid of chemicals produced
50 by strong feelings.

    In the United States men have heart disease more often than women do. Doctors say heart disease and some other diseases are related to the pressures of living and working in a modern society. Perhaps men suffer more
55 from these diseases because they do not cry enough. And it is possible that as more and more women work outside the home, they will also suffer from more pressure. Then everyone will need to cry more.

I. VOCABULARY

sorrow	fault	embarrassed	final
competition	poison	rudely	bursts
death	announced	judges	chemicals
boss	terrible	suffer	tears
places	couple		

1. A couple is going to come into the office this afternoon to sign the _____ papers.
2. Then her _____ calls her into his office.
3. The boss is very angry and speaks _____ to Mary.
4. She knows it is not her _____.
5. She _____ into tears.
6. In Atlantic City the Miss America _____ is nearly finished.
7. The _____ choose Miss Alabama as _____ the most beautiful woman in the United States.
8. She steps forward, and the outgoing Miss America _____ a crown on her head.
9. People cry when something _____ happens.
10. They cry in _____ when a close friend has a death in the family.
11. Mary was _____ and very angry with herself.

12. Chemists say the body produces two kinds of _____.
13. When people cry because of their feelings, these tears have _____ chemicals in them.
14. The body is getting rid of _____ produced by strong feelings.
15. Perhaps men _____ more from heart disease because they do not cry enough.

II. VOCABULARY (new context)

boss	sorrow	judge	chemicals
embarrassed	fault	finalists	rude
places	suffered	burst	announced
competition	couple	yard	terrible

1. War brings _____ and destruction to the countries that are fighting.
2. There are two _____ in the race. This last race will decide the winner.
3. Larry was very _____ when he could not remember his teacher's name. His face turned red.
4. The President _____ today that there will be a national conference on energy.
5. _____ are made from petroleum in petrochemical factories.
6. The _____ gave her workers a special holiday last month.
7. The _____ decided the man should go to prison for twenty years because he poisoned his wife.
8. There was a _____ accident when a plane took off at the airport. Over 200 people were killed.
9. A dog was run over by a car. It _____ so much from the pain that the owner had to kill it.
10. Something that is polite in one country may seem _____ in another.
11. It's my _____ that the dinner burned. I was talking on the telephone and forgot that the food was cooking.
12. Ellen won first prize in the science _____ at her school. She had the most interesting experiment.
13. A dam _____ and flooded the area.
14. A trapper usually _____ his trap near a beaver dam or house.

III. VOCABULARY REVIEW

Match each word with its meaning. Write the letter of the meaning by the word that it means.

1. printed
2. border
3. forever
4. so far
5. wildlife
6. no longer
7. mud
8. religion
9. sheep
10. perfume

a. always
b. a mixture of dirt and water
c. not anymore
d. written in a newspaper or book
e. something to fly with
f. wild animals
g. the division between two countries
h. something that smells very nice
i. until now
j. a system of beliefs about God
k. ride on the water
l. an animal that produces wool

IV. ORAL QUESTIONS

1. Why did Mary cry?
2. Why did Paul cry?
3. Why did Miss America cry?
4. Why do people cry in general?
5. How are people changing their ideas about crying?
6. What do chemists say about tears?
7. What do doctors say about heart disease and modern society?
*8. As developing countries modernize, what will probably happen to the amount of heart disease? Why?

V. COMPREHENSION

1. Mary cried in her boss's office because she felt _____.
   a. excited
   b. helpless
   c. better
   d. happy
2. Paul cried because of his _____.
   a. rudeness
   b. embarrassment
   c. fright
   d. sorrow

3. Miss America cried because she was so _____.
   a. happy   c. angry
   b. sorrowful   d. helpless
4. People cry when they feel very bad and when they feel very _____.
   a. polite   c. smooth
   b. good   d. strong
5. Men are beginning to realize that it is all right to _____.
   a. have heart attacks   c. show their feelings
   b. sell houses   d. drink poison chemicals
6. Heart disease is related to _____.
   a. the pressures of a modern society
   b. frightening children
   c. being a finalist
   d. being in a public place

VI. MAIN IDEA

Choose the three main ideas.

_____ 1. Mary felt ashamed and angry with herself after she cried in her boss's office.
_____ 2. People cry when they feel bad and when they feel good.
_____ 3. Chemists say the body produces two different kinds of tears.
_____ 4. Perhaps men suffer from more diseases because they do not cry enough.
_____ 5. People cry when something wonderful happens.

WORD STUDY

I. PREPOSITIONS

Write the correct preposition in each blank.

1. Mary sells houses _____ a large company.
2. A couple has agreed to buy a house _____ $150,000.

3. Then her boss calls her _____ his office.
4. She was planning _____ buy a new car.
5. Paul is sitting _____ the backyard _____ his wife and children.
6. It is Paul's mother calling _____ another city.
7. People cry when they have been very worried _____ something but find _____ everything is all right.
8. Mary was very angry _____ herself because she cried _____ her boss's office.
9. _____ the United States _____ lately men were not supposed _____ cry.
10. Women are learning that sometimes they can do something _____ a problem instead _____ just crying.

II. IRREGULAR VERBS

Learn these verbs. Put the correct form in each sentence.

Present	Past	Past Participle
lose	lost	lost
burst	burst	burst
ring	rang	rung
spread	spread	spread
win	won	won
fight	fought	fought

1. Ali _____ his passport yesterday.
2. Two men _____ through the crowd, talking excitedly.
3. Has the bell _____ yet?
4. A new kind of popular music _____ quickly from country to country.
5. Who _____ the football game?
6. The French and English _____ over the best areas for trapping beavers.

III. CONTEXT CLUES

1. Helen sold David a car. They signed the papers, but David never paid Helen any money. Now they are fighting over the ownership of the car.
   a. who bought   c. who owns
   b. who sold   d. who signs

2. Ms. Davis is <u>attempting</u> to learn how to play the piano. She practices two hours a day and has a lesson *every week*.
   a. trying
   b. attacking
   c. placing
   d. judging
3. Pierre failed the exam even though it was very easy. <u>Obviously</u>, he did not study.
   a. It is easy to find time to study.
   b. It is easy to see or understand.
   c. The exam was easy.
   d. Whether
4. In 1776 thirteen British colonies <u>united</u> to form the United States of America.
   a. country
   b. repaired
   c. joined together
   d. separated
5. Mary <u>craves</u> attention. She talks loudly and wears bright-colored clothes. She asks lots of questions in class.
   a. pays
   b. wants very much
   c. puts
   d. cuts from a piece of ivory

THE UNITED NATIONS

In 1945 leaders from fifty-one countries met in San Francisco and organized the United Nations (UN). World War II had just ended. Millions of people had died, and there was destruction everywhere. People hoped they
5 could build a future of world peace with this new organization.

The United Nations has four main goals and purposes:

   1. To work together for international peace and to solve international problems
10   2. To develop friendly relations among nations
   3. To work together for human rights for everyone of all races, religions, languages, and of both sexes
   4. To build a center where nations can work together for these goals

15 Today almost every country in the world is a member of the UN. Each country has signed an agreement that says:

   1. All members are equal.
   2. All members promise to solve international prob-
20   lems in a peaceful way.
   3. No member will use <u>force</u> against another member.   (strength, power)
   4. All members will help the UN in its actions.
   5. The UN will not try to solve problems within countries except to enforce international peace.

25 Obviously, the United Nations has not been completely successful in its goals. There have been several wars since 1945. However, the organization has helped bring

Headquarters of the United Nations
United Nations, New York

peace to some countries that were at war. It has helped
people who left their countries because of wars. It has
30 helped bring independence to colonies.

The main United Nations organization in New York
City has a "family" of other organizations. These organizations try to provide a better life for everyone. For example, UNICEF, the organization for children, provides
35 food, medical care, and many other services to poor children. The World Health Organization develops medical
programs all over the world.

There are thousands of UN workers in developing
countries. They work as planners to increase production
40 in farming and industry. They provide medical services,
improve education programs, and spread scientific information. They develop programs that provide jobs and
better living conditions. They help countries control their
population growth.

45 The United Nations also holds large international conferences. One was on the uses and ownership of oceans.
Another was on women. There are also International
Years to work on special problems. One year was the International Year of the Child.

50 For centuries countries have fought each other, and
powerful countries have taken control of weaker ones. It
is very difficult to persuade nations to live together in
peace. Nevertheless, the United Nations is <u>attempting</u> to   (trying)
do this. It is the only organization that <u>unites</u> the world in   (joins together)
55 the search for peace. If it is successful, it will bring a
better life for all humanity.

I. VOCABULARY

unites	enforce	force	purposes
ownership	obviously	attempting	religions

1. The United Nations has four main goals and _____.
2. No member will use _____ against another member.
3. The UN will not try to solve problems within countries except to
   _____ international peace.

4. _____, the United Nations has not been completely successful in its goals.
5. One conference was on the uses and _____ of oceans.
6. Nevertheless, the United Nations is _____ to persuade nations to live together in peace.
7. It is the only organization that _____ the world in the search for peace.

II. VOCABULARY (new context)

united	force	ownership
enforce	purpose	search
for example	success	obviously

1. Governments make laws. Police _____ laws.
2. What is the _____ of a canal? Why do people build canals?
3. Canada and the _____ States are both in North America.
4. Antarctica is almost all covered with ice. It is _____ very cold there.
5. I lost the key to my apartment and had to _____ the lock to open the door.
6. Think carefully before buying a house. _____ of a house can be very expensive.

III. VOCABULARY REVIEW: Antonyms

Match each word or phrase with one that means the opposite.

1. final
2. rude
3. sorrow
4. terrible
5. damage
6. so far
7. all over
8. huge

a. happiness
b. from now on
c. repair
d. first
e. tiny
f. burst
g. polite
h. fault
i. nowhere
j. wonderful
k. nearby

IV. ORAL QUESTIONS

1. Why was the United Nations formed?
2. What are the four goals and purposes of the United Nations?
3. What five things do United Nations members agree to?
4. How has the United Nations been unsuccessful? Successful?
5. What kind of work does the United Nations "family" of organizations do?
6. What else does the United Nations do?
*7. Why are there wars even though United Nations members agree not to fight?
*8. What do you think people talked about at the conference on oceans?

V. COMPREHENSION

Write *T* if the statement is true.
Write *F* if the statement is false.
Write *NI* if there is no information about the statement.

_____ 1. The United Nations was organized in San Francisco.
_____ 2. Canada was at the meeting in San Francisco.
_____ 3. The United Nations works for international peace.
_____ 4. Kuwait is a member of the United Nations.
_____ 5. A small country is equal to a large country in the United Nations.
_____ 6. The United Nations has brought peace to the world.
_____ 7. The United Nations helped Algeria become independent.
_____ 8. United Nations workers help Japanese television factories increase production.

VI. MAIN IDEA

Choose the two main ideas.

_____ 1. The United Nations was organized in San Francisco by fifty-one countries.
_____ 2. UNICEF is the United Nations organization for children, and the World Health Organization does medical work.

‾‾‾‾‾ 3. The United Nations works for world peace and human rights.

‾‾‾‾‾ 4. The United Nations helps developing countries and holds international conferences.

WORD STUDY

I. SUFFIXES: Nouns ending in -ship

The ending -ship means the condition of or the art of.

> Examples: One United Nations conference was on the uses and ownership of oceans. (It was about who owns the oceans.)
>
> Japanese students usually have excellent penmanship. (They write each word carefully and beautifully.)

Add *-ship* to each of these words. Then choose the right word for each sentence. One word is plural.

member   hard   sportsman   friend   relation

1. People who play sports should follow the rules of the game and be friendly to the other team. This is good ‾‾‾‾‾‾‾‾‾‾.
2. The early explorers in Antarctica suffered many ‾‾‾‾‾‾‾‾‾‾. It was terribly cold, and sometimes they did not have enough supplies. Some of them died.
3. The ‾‾‾‾‾‾‾‾‾‾ of the International Students Organization is now 125. Last year there were 100 members.
4. Marie and Anne became friends in school. Now they are grandmothers, and they are still friends. Their ‾‾‾‾‾‾‾‾‾‾ is still very important to them.
5. What is the ‾‾‾‾‾‾‾‾‾‾ between goats and deserts? How do goats cause deserts to become larger?

II. PREFIXES: Verbs with en-

Example: The police sometimes use force to <u>enforce</u> the law.

Write *en-* at the beginning of each word. Then choose the right word for each sentence. (Use the correct tense.)

joy   circle   rich   large   danger

1. Some whaling companies _____ themselves by selling whale meat at very high prices.
2. The army made a circle around the enemy during the night. After they had _____ the enemy, they attacked.
3. The Browns _____ their visit to Yellowstone National Park last year.
4. Canada has _____ its national park system over the years. It has added new parks to make the system larger.
5. A beaver dam _____ the trees behind it. As the water rises, it can kill the trees.

III. CONTEXT CLUES

1. Our house has a <u>storage room</u> next to the garage. It is full of suitcases, things we use to repair the house, our children's old toys, a box of dishes we never use, and all kinds of other things.
   a. a place to buy things
   b. a living room
   c. a place to keep things we do not often use
   d. a place to sleep
2. When you ride a motorcycle, you should wear a <u>helmet</u>. Then if you have an accident, you will not hurt your head.
   a. strong, high shoes
   b. a hard hat to protect your head
   c. something to keep you warm in winter
   d. something to protect your hands
3. Here is an easy way to cook an egg. Put the egg in very hot water and <u>boil</u> it for three minutes.
   a. fry
   b. cook at 100°C.
   c. cook slowly in warm water
   d. cook in oil

4. It is very hot today. <u>What is the</u> <u>temperature?</u> It is 38°C.
   a. How hot (or cold) is it?
   b. What time is it?
   c. How fast is it?
   d. How far is it?
5. The test tomorrow will have ten words from this lesson. It will have ten <u>additional</u> words from other lessons. There will be twenty words on the test.
   a. difficult
   b. easy
   c. less
   d. more

MAPLE SYRUP

People like sweet food, and for centuries they have used sugar and honey as sweeteners. The Indians in eastern Canada and the eastern United States learned to

make a sweetener from the sap, or sweet water, from the
5 maple tree.

There are several kinds of maple trees, but the sugar
maple grows only in the northeastern United States and
in eastern Canada. (There is a maple leaf on the Canadian
flag.) The maple is a large tree that grows up to thirty
10 meters high. In the autumn the leaves turn red and orange
before they fall from the trees.

In late February or early March after several sunny
days and cold, dry nights, the sap starts running through
the trees. The Indians made a small hole in each tree, put
15 in a small spout, and hung a pail on the spout. The sap
ran slowly through the spout into the pail. As each small
pail filled, the Indians poured the sap into larger pails
and then boiled it over a fire for a long time. As the sap
boiled, it became thicker and thicker, sweeter and sweeter,
20 until it was a thick syrup. The sap is like water, and it takes
from thirty to fifty liters of sap to make a liter of maple
syrup.

When Europeans started coming to North America,
the Indians taught them how to make maple syrup. In the
25 eighteenth and nineteenth centuries, it was an important
food crop. It was important in commerce until sugar became cheaper. Then people started using sugar as a
sweetener.

For 300 years people used the traditional method of
30 making maple syrup. Some people continue to make it
the old way, but most people who gather sap as a commercial crop use a modern system. Plastic pipes go directly from each tree to large storage tanks. More pipes take
the sap to a large sugarhouse, where it is boiled.
35 Maple syrup is served mostly on pancakes for break-
fast. It is also used in candy and ice cream and made into
maple sugar and maple butter.

Maple syrup is one of the oldest crops in North America. It is also one of the very few crops that are produced
40 only in North America and nowhere else in the world.

I. VOCABULARY

tanks	maple	commerce	boiled
pail	thick	sweetener	syrup
sap	poured	spout	honey
plastic	thin	storage	pipes

1. For centuries people have used sugar and _____ as sweeteners.
2. Indians learned to make a sweetener from _____.
3. This sap comes from the _____ tree.
4. The Indians made a small hole in each tree and put in a small _____.
5. They hung a _____ on the spout.
6. The Indians _____ the sap into larger pails.
7. Then they _____ it over a fire for a long time.
8. As the sap boiled, it became a thick _____.
9. Plastic pipes go directly from each tree to large _____.
10. More _____ take the sap to a large sugarhouse.

II. VOCABULARY (new context)

pipe	tank	storage
pour	honey	syrup
boils	spout	maple
pails		

1. Carol will leave her bicycle in her friend's _____ room during
   the summer.
2. Chocolate _____ on ice cream is very good.
3. Please _____ some more coffee into my cup.
4. A huge _____ carries petroleum across Alaska. It is called a
   pipeline.
5. _____ trees are beautiful in the fall.
6. A car has a gas _____ to hold the gas.
7. _____ is used in several desserts in the Middle East.
8. Paul used ten _____ of water when he washed his car.
9. Water _____ at 100°C. (° = degree)

III. VOCABULARY REVIEW

entire	sorrow	pond	sharp
place	fault	tears	warning
preparing	value	judges	embarrassing

1. The _____ chose the best composition in the competition.
2. Whose _____ is it that the sports equipment isn't ready?
3. It is _____ to break a glass in a restaurant.
4. Ms. Hill is _____ dinner now.
5. The child cried so hard that _____ were running down her face.
6. The _____ class is here today.
7. The students with bad grades received a _____ letter.
8. What is the _____ of gold now?

IV. ORAL QUESTIONS

1. Name two common sweeteners.
2. Describe the maple tree.
3. What kind of weather is necessary to make maple syrup?
4. Explain the traditional method of making maple syrup.
*5. Why was maple syrup important in commerce in the eighteenth and nineteenth centuries?
6. Explain the modern way to make maple syrup.
7. How is maple syrup used today?

V. COMPREHENSION: True/False/No Information (T/F/NI)

_____ 1. The Indians used honey as a sweetener.
_____ 2. The sugar maple tree grows only in eastern Canada and the northeastern United States.
_____ 3. Hot weather makes the sap start to run in maple trees.
_____ 4. The sap becomes thicker as it boils.
_____ 5. Germans were the first Europeans to make maple syrup.
_____ 6. People who make maple syrup commercially modernized the production system.
_____ 7. Maple syrup is only one of many unusual crops in North America.

VI. MAIN IDEA

Choose the two main ideas.

_____ 1. Indians developed a method for making maple sugar.
_____ 2. People use sugar as a sweetener.
_____ 3. Maple syrup was important in commerce in the eighteenth and nineteenth centuries.
_____ 4. Today maple syrup is made by both the traditional and modern methods.
_____ 5. There are several kinds of maple trees.

WORD STUDY

I. SUFFIXES: Nouns Ending in -age

> Example: There is a <u>passage</u> between those two buildings. In winter people can pass or walk through this narrow hall without going outside.

Add *-age* to each word. Then choose the right word for each sentence.
Spelling: Change the final *y* to *i*. Drop the final *e*.

marry	store	post
short	out	pack

1. Alice and Paul got married when they were twenty. After five years of _____, they got divorced.
2. There was very bad weather in Brazil, and most of the coffee crop was destroyed. Now the supermarkets in the United States are short of coffee. They do not have enough coffee to sell because of this _____.
3. Louis bought several presents for his parents. He packed them carefully in a box. Then he took the _____ to the post office and mailed it.

4. How much _____ do you need for an airmail letter to Saudi Arabia? You can find out at the post office.
5. There was an electrical storm last night, and the electricity went out. No one could turn on the lights. The _____ lasted for three hours.
6. Our apartment building has a _____ room. It is for things that people do not use very often.

II. SUFFIXES: Nouns Ending in -ist (a person)

Example: A <u>chemist</u> is a person who works in chemistry.

Put the right word in each sentence. Use the plural if it is necessary.

artist	naturalist	zoologist	guitarist
pianist	scientist	finalist	

1. Two teams are playing the last games for the World Cup. One of these _____ will win the competition.
2. Some country musicians are excellent _____. They sing and play the guitar.
3. Picasso was a famous _____.
4. Carol is interested in animals and wants to become a _____.
5. Mr. Taylor studied piano for twenty years and became a famous _____.
6. _____ give talks at national parks.
7. Albert Einstein was a famous _____.

III. CONTEXT CLUES

1. Carl wants to work for a national company that sells farm equipment. He wants a good job in the main office, so he is going to study <u>marketing</u>.
   a. supermarkets   c. buying
   b. solving   d. buying and selling
2. Coffee, orange juice, and petroleum are all <u>liquids</u>. Ice becomes a <u>liquid</u> at 0°C.
   a. something that provides energy   c. water
   b. something that can be poured   d. something to drink

3. Please put the dishes in the <u>cupboard</u> in the kitchen. Then close the <u>cupboard</u> doors.
   a. a place to keep things
   b. something to drink from
   c. something to eat from
   d. a kind of dining room
4. Don is interested in bushes and other plants that grow in hot countries. He plans to study <u>botany</u>.
   a. the science of animals
   b. farming
   c. buying and selling
   d. the science of plants
5. Kenya, Indonesia, Ecuador, and Brazil are all on the <u>equator</u>.
   a. an imaginary line near Antarctica
   b. an imaginary line around the center of the earth
   c. equal
   d. a famous river

BE CAREFUL IN
THE SUPERMARKET!

How do you decide what you are going to buy in a supermarket? Do you look in the refrigerator and the kitchen cupboards and make a list? Do you think about

what you want to cook and then buy the food you need?
5 Even if you do these things, the supermarket makes some
of the <u>decisions</u> for you. (noun for decide)

Specialists in <u>marketing</u> have studied how to make (buying and selling)
people buy more food in a supermarket. They do all
kinds of things that you do not even notice. For example,
10 the simple, ordinary food that everybody must buy, like
bread, milk, flour, and vegetable oil, is spread all over the
store. You have to walk by all the more interesting—and
more expensive—things in order to find what you need.
The more expensive food is in packages with bright-
15 colored pictures. This food is placed at eye level so you
see it and want to buy it. The things that you have to buy
anyway are usually located on a higher or lower shelf.
However, candy and other things that children like are on
lower shelves. One study showed that when a super-
20 market moved four products from floor to eye level, it
sold 78 percent more.

Another study showed that for every minute a person
is in a supermarket after the first half hour, she or he
spends $.50. If someone stays forty minutes, the super-
25 market has an additional $5.00. So the store has a com-
fortable temperature in summer and winter, and it plays
soft music. It is a pleasant place for people to stay—and
spend more money.

Supermarkets also sell a few things at a lower, or special,
30 price every week. Some people think this means all the
prices are lower. Some of these "specials" are not really
cheaper. Something that is usually $.50, might be a "spe-
cial" at 2/$1.00 (two for a dollar). Or something that is
not selling very fast at $.29 is put on "special" at 2/60¢.
35 People think it is cheaper and buy it.

Some stores have red or pink lights over the meat so
the meat looks redder. They put light green paper around
lettuce and put apples in red plastic bags.

So be careful in the supermarket. You may go home
40 with a bag of food you were not planning to buy. The
supermarket, not you, decided you should buy it.

I. VOCABULARY

decisions	flour	plastic	lettuce
candy	cupboards	marketing	additional
pleasant	shelf	temperature	anyway

1. Do you look in the refrigerator and kitchen _____ and make a list?
2. The supermarket makes some of the _____ for you.
3. Specialists in _____ have studied how to make people buy more food.
4. The simple food that everybody must buy, like bread, milk, and _____, is spread all over the store.
5. The things that you have to buy _____ are usually placed on a higher or lower _____.
6. However, _____ and other things children like are on lower shelves.
7. The store has a comfortable _____ in summer and winter.
8. If someone stays forty minutes, the supermarket has an _____ $5.00.
9. Stores put light green paper around _____.

II. VOCABULARY (new context)

lettuce	anyway	temperature	flour
candy	pleasant	additional	decision
marketing	cupboard	specialist	shelf

1. _____ has sugar, corn syrup, or sometimes maple sugar in it as a sweetener.
2. The flour is on the bottom _____ in the _____.
3. Think carefully before you decide. This is an important _____.
4. Sudbury sometimes has the lowest _____ in Canada. It is a very cold city.
5. Mark does not need any more shoes, but he is going to buy some _____.
6. Salad is often made with _____ and tomatoes.
7. _____ can be made from wheat, rice, corn, or other plants.

8. _____ is almost a science in the United States. Specialists can persuade people to buy almost anything.

9. This paper explains how to get a passport. If you need any _____ information, telephone the passport office.

III. VOCABULARY REVIEW

Match the word with the correct meaning.

1. obvious	a. a sweetener
2. unite	b. easy to see
3. attempt	c. competition
4. honey	d. join together
5. boil	e. place
6. rude	f. last
7. final	g. not polite
8. locate	h. try
	i. heat to 100°C.
	j. purpose

IV. ORAL QUESTIONS

1. Why is simple food spread all over the supermarket?
2. What kinds of food do they put at eye level? Why?
*3. Why is candy on a lower shelf?
*4. Rice and beans are usually in an uninteresting plastic bag. Why?
5. Why does a supermarket play soft music?
*6. Why do some stores have apples in red plastic bags?
*7. Why do some supermarkets have chocolate syrup by the ice cream?

V. COMPREHENSION

1. Marketing specialists study _____.
   a. the ownership of supermarkets
   b. how to build cupboards
   c. plants suitable for human needs
   d. methods of selling more products

2. The more expensive food is _____.
   a. on high shelves
   b. in bright-colored packages
   c. all near the front of the store
   d. usually on special

*3. If someone is in the supermarket for an hour, he or she probably spends an additional _____.
   a. $10
   b. $15
   c. $20
   d. $30

4. A "special" _____.
   a. is sometimes more expensive
   b. is always cheaper
   c. always means the price is lower
   d. means everything is at a special price

*5. A good way to save money in a supermarket is to _____.
   a. make a list of what you need before you go
   b. go just before dinner
   c. walk around and see what you need
   d. buy things that are in the prettiest packages

*6. Children's books are probably _____ in a supermarket.
   a. on special most of the time
   b. on high shelves
   c. on low shelves
   d. spread all over the store

VI. MAIN IDEA

Choose the one main idea.

_____ 1. The location of a product helps sell it.
_____ 2. Marketing specialists use all kinds of methods to sell products.
_____ 3. Some "specials" are not special at all.
_____ 4. Soft music and a comfortable temperature help sell products.

WORD STUDY

I. WORD FORMS

Verb	Noun	Adjective
1. compete	competition	competitive
2.	chemical	chemical
	chemist	
3. poison	poison	poison
		poisonous
4. embarrass	embarrassment	embarrassed
5. announce	announcement	
6. unite	union	united
7. store	storage	
8. decide	decision	
9. add	addition	additional
10. refrigerate	refrigeration	
	refrigerator	

Write the correct word form in the sentence. Use the right verb tense, and use singular or plural nouns.

1. Tom is very _____. He always wants to win or be the best.
2. Petro_____ are made from petroleum.
3. Mice can be killed with traps or _____.
4. Susan's face turned red because she was _____.
5. The president of the university made an important _____ to the students.
6. USSR stands for the _____ of Soviet Socialist Republics.
7. Mr. and Mrs. Walker are going to work in Mexico for a year. They will _____ their furniture while they are gone.
8. You must make a _____ about renting this apartment right away. Someone else wants it, too.
9. A beaver _____ more sticks and mud to its dam when it is necessary.
10. _____ is necessary to keep some kinds of medicine fresh.

II. NOUN SUBSTITUTES

Look at these words in the reading selection. Then tell what each word means.

1. Page 171   line 8, they
2.   line 16, it
3.   line 23, she or he
4.   line 27, it
5.   line 35, it
6.   line 41, it

III. CONTEXT CLUES

1. Whalers travel to <u>distant</u> oceans in search of whales. They go to Antarctica and the Arctic.
   - a. unpopulated
   - b. international
   - c. frightening
   - d. far away
2. Mary had to <u>rush</u> to the supermarket to get there before it closed.
   - a. hurry
   - b. run
   - c. push the door open
   - d. go shopping
3. Large companies <u>mine</u> gold in South Africa.
   - a. not yours
   - b. store
   - c. take out of the ground
   - d. enforce
4. The program starts at 7:00 and <u>lasts</u> an hour.
   - a. not first
   - b. continues
   - c. ends
   - d. final
5. The police officer <u>seized</u> the man's arm and made him drop the knife.
   - a. took hold of
   - b. shot
   - c. poured
   - d. persuaded

GLASS

Glass is everywhere in our lives. It is so common that we hardly think about it. We look through it when we look out the window and if we wear glasses. We drink from it and sometimes eat from it. The light in our homes

5 comes through glass windows in the daytime and from glass lights at night. Glass is used in homes, schools, businesses, industry, and automobiles.

Fortunately for us, glass is made from very inexpensive materials. The main material is sand from quartz rock.
10 The mixture is heated until it becomes a syrupy liquid. When the liquid cools, it becomes glass.

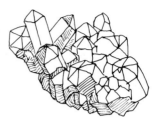

No one knows who first discovered glass or how. Early humans used obsidian, a natural glass formed by volcanoes, to make tools and jewelry. People probably began
15 making glass themselves around 3000 B.C. in Syria. Then in a war between Egypt and Syria in 1400 B.C., Syria became part of Egypt. The Egyptians took Syrian glassmakers back to Egypt, and over the centuries the entire eastern Mediterranean area became a glassmaking center.

20 Probably around 300 B.C. the blowpipe was invented. Egyptian glassmakers developed the use of the blowpipe. They specialized in beautiful jewelry, dishes, and other containers. Egyptian glass became so famous that in 26 B.C. Emperor Augustus announced that Egypt had to pay
25 its taxes to Rome with glass.

The Romans soon started making their own glass. Then they realized that glass could be used to make windows. A few centuries later, Europeans made magnificent church windows from colored glass.
30 Slowly methods of glassmaking improved, and glassmakers were able to lower prices. Nevertheless, until about 1900 glass was still made in the traditional ways with very few changes.

Since 1900 companies have developed many new
35 types of glass. Safety glass is a sandwich of glass and plastic. If it breaks, the pieces stay together instead of flying in all directions. This invention is very useful in automobile windows. One kind of glass stops most of the heat from the sun. It is widely used in buildings. Another kind is like
40 a mirror from one side. From the other side it is like a window.

Some windows are made from two sheets of glass with air trapped in a space between them. This helps keep out the heat and cold. Glass can also trap the heat of the sun

45 to heat a building. Laboratory glass can be heated to high
temperatures without breaking. One of the most interesting kinds of glass is used in banks and jewelry stores. It
is made of glass and plastic but looks like ordinary glass.
If someone shoots a gun, the bullet cannot go through
50 the glass.

    Today most glass is made by machines in large fac-
tories. No one touches it. People use television and computers to control the machines. Nevertheless, a few glass-
blowers still take pleasure in making glass the traditional
55 way. They make beautiful containers and jewelry just as
the Egyptians did.

I. VOCABULARY

tools	emperor	quartz	form
obsidian	sheets	bullet	volcanoes
invented	types	liquid	temperature

1. The main material in glass is sand from _____ rock.
2. The mixture is heated until it becomes a syrupy _____.
3. Early humans used _____, a natural glass formed by _____, to make _____ and jewelry.
4. Probably around 300 B.C. the blowpipe was _____.
5. In 26 B.C. _____ Augustus announced that Egypt had to pay its taxes to Rome with glass.
6. Since 1900 companies have developed many new _____ of glass.
7. Some windows are made from two _____ of glass.
8. If someone shoots a gun, the _____ cannot go through the glass.

II. VOCABULARY (new context)

invented	volcano	emperor	tools	sheet
types	liquid	bullet	heat	laboratory

1. Napoleon was a famous _____.
2. Superman is faster than a speeding _____.

3. Several _____ of plants contain protein.
4. An electrician uses different types of _____ at work.
5. Hawaii has an active _____ that shoots liquid rock into the air.
6. Thomas Edison _____ the electric light.
7. Please lend me a _____ of paper.
8. A _____ becomes a gas when it boils.

III. VOCABULARY REVIEW

Match each word with its meaning.

1. explode	a. get ready
2. tank	b. a container for liquids
3. prepare	c. whole
4. float	d. burst
5. knock over	e. shelf
6. entire	f. pipe
7. marketing	g. make something fall
	h. ride on water
	i. buying and selling

IV. ORAL QUESTIONS

1. How is glass made?
2. Where does obsidian come from?
3. How did Egyptians learn to make glass?
4. What is a blowpipe?
5. Who discovered how to make glass windows?
6. Describe some types of glass used in buildings.
7. How is glass made today?

V. COMPREHENSION

1. We hardly think about glass because _____.
   a. it is made from inexpensive materials
   b. it is clear
   c. we can see through it
   d. it is so common

2. Today glass is made mainly from _____.
   a. obsidian
   b. quartz sand
   c. tools
   d. a syrupy liquid
3. A method of making glass was probably first discovered in _____.
   a. Syria
   b. Egypt
   c. Europe
   d. Rome
4. Glass windows were invented by _____.
   a. Syrians
   b. Egyptians
   c. Europeans
   d. Romans
5. Glassmaking methods did not change much until _____.
   a. Egyptians began making glass
   b. Europeans made church windows
   c. the twentieth century
   d. Romans invented windows

VI. MAIN IDEA

Choose the three main ideas.

_____ 1. The history of glass
_____ 2. Types of modern glass
_____ 3. Types of glass in buildings
_____ 4. Methods of making glass
_____ 5. Egyptian methods of making glass

WORD STUDY

I. SUFFIXES: Noun + y = Adjective

Add y to a noun to make an adjective.

Example: The mixture is heated until it becomes a <u>syrupy</u> liquid.
Spelling: Use the 1−1−1 rule.
        Drop the final <u>e</u>.

Add *y* to each word. Then use the right word in each sentence.

Noun	Adjective	Noun	Adjective	Noun	Adjective	Noun	Adjective
sun	_____	juice	_____	wind	_____	ice	_____
mud	_____	dirt	_____	cloud	_____	rain	_____

1. Yesterday the wind started to blow and it started to rain. The weather was _____ and _____ all night.
2. Today the weather is warm and _____.
3. A banana is not _____.

II. SUFFIXES: Nouns Ending in *-y, -ty, -ity*

It is common to change an adjective to a noun by adding -y, -ty, or -ity.

Write the noun for each adjective. Then choose the best word for each sentence. Use a plural noun if necessary.

<table>
<tr><td colspan="2" align="center">-y</td><td colspan="2" align="center">-ty</td></tr>
<tr><td>Adjective</td><td>Noun</td><td>Adjective</td><td>Noun</td></tr>
<tr><td>difficult</td><td>_____</td><td>certain</td><td>_____</td></tr>
<tr><td></td><td></td><td>safe</td><td>_____</td></tr>
<tr><td></td><td></td><td>special</td><td>_____</td></tr>
</table>

<table>
<tr><td colspan="2" align="center">-ity</td></tr>
<tr><td>Adjective</td><td>Noun</td></tr>
<tr><td>able</td><td>ability</td></tr>
<tr><td>electric</td><td></td></tr>
<tr><td>equal</td><td></td></tr>
<tr><td>popular</td><td></td></tr>
<tr><td>human</td><td></td></tr>
<tr><td>similar</td><td></td></tr>
</table>

1. Computers are changing the lives of all _____.
2. Blacks in the United States have been working for _____ for three centuries.
3. Factories should provide _____ equipment for the workers. This would help prevent accidents.
4. Third world governments have _____ in providing services for their cities.

5. The _____ of this restaurant is rich desserts.
6. There are several _____ between the Antarctic and the Arctic Oceans.
7. The beaver has the _____ to build dams.

III. CONTEXT CLUES

1. People have used glass <u>throughout</u> history.
   a. destroyed
   b. everywhere
   c. by
   d. during all of
2. The Rockefellers earned a <u>fortune</u> producing oil.
   a. good luck
   b. a lot of money
   c. bad luck
   d. a million dollars
3. A stone <u>sinks</u> in water. Wood floats.
   a. falls to the bottom
   b. floats
   c. is washed
   d. becomes brighter-colored
4. In <u>ancient times</u> the Egyptians learned glassmaking from the Syrians.
   a. several times
   b. a long time ago
   c. in a short time
   d. shortly
5. Large <u>quantities</u> of glass are used to make windows.
   a. pieces
   b. sheets
   c. qualities
   d. amounts

GOLD

Throughout history gold has been important in human society. Men have killed for it. People have suffered great hardships searching for it. They have gone to the distant corners of the earth hoping to find a great fortune. The

(during all)

(far)

5 Spanish explored a new world in search of it. They used
great cruelty toward the Indians who worked in the mines.
The ancient Egyptians were also very cruel to their miners.
A kind of madness <u>seizes</u> people when they think about   (takes hold of)
gold.

10   Gold probably came up from great depths in the earth
mixed with other minerals. It was at least partly in liquid
form. It is found most often mixed with quartz and iron,
but it is found in at least tiny <u>quantities</u> in all rocks.   (amounts)

For centuries starting in ancient times gold was most
15 commonly found mixed with sand in streams. This is one
reason why even early humans used it. They could find it
without using tools to dig it out of the ground. It was also
valuable to them because it is very soft. It is one of the
softest metals and also one of the heaviest. It is easy to
20 work into jewelry and other decorations. It is beautiful
and lasts forever. Gold leaf, a thin sheet of gold, can be
made so thin that light shines through it.

Remains of ancient gold mines have been found in
Egypt. These are the earliest mines anyone has found so
25 far. After the discovery of America, most of the world's
gold was produced there. Now South Africa leads the
world in gold production.

It is very easy to separate gold from the sand in a river.
Just put some of the sand and water in a pan. Shake it
30 and the gold sinks to the bottom. Pour off some of the
sand and water. Then add more water, shake it, and pour
it off again. Continue this until nothing remains but the
gold.

In recent times there have been several gold rushes.
35 People heard stories of finding large pieces of gold lying
on the ground. Or they heard they could earn a fortune
just by digging a little. Then all kinds of people rushed to
the location of the latest gold discovery.

The California gold rush starting in 1849 brought hun-
40 dreds of people into a wild, unknown area with very
little government control. Most of them were very independent and looking for adventure as well as riches. The
gold rush on the Fraser River in British Columbia was
different. The miners needed a license from the Canadian

45 government and were not free to move around the area
to look for gold.

There were other gold rushes in Canada, the United
States, Australia, and New Zealand. In 1886 gold was discovered in South Africa. However, the situation was dif-
50 ferent there. The miners needed complicated machinery
to take gold from the ground and separate it from the
other minerals. Only large companies had the money to
do this. For this reason, a few large mining companies
control the gold production in South Africa today.
55 Gold lasts forever. For centuries people have made
gold coins and jewelry, later melted them into a liquid,
and used the gold again. If you have some gold jewelry,
it is possible that this same gold was a piece of jewelry for
someone who lived thousands of years ago. And thou-
60 sands of years from now, someone else may be wearing
this same gold in another form.

I. VOCABULARY

sinks	melted	ancient	chain	tears
decorations	madness	fortune	distant	cruelty
throughout	lasts	minerals	seizes	rushes
license	situation	quantities	mines	computers

1. _____ history gold has been important in human society.
2. People have gone to the _____ corners of the earth hoping
   to find a great _____.
3. The Spanish used great _____ toward the Indians who
   worked in the _____.
4. The _____ Egyptians were also very cruel to their miners.
5. A kind of _____ _____ people when they think
   about gold.
6. Gold was probably carried up from great depths in the earth mixed with
   other _____.
7. It is found in at least tiny _____ in all rocks.
8. It is easy to work into jewelry and other _____.
9. It is beautiful and _____ forever.

10. Put sand and water in a pan. The gold ＿＿＿＿＿＿ to the bottom.
11. In recent times there have been several gold ＿＿＿＿＿＿.
12. The miners needed a ＿＿＿＿＿＿ from the Canadian government.
13. However, the ＿＿＿＿＿＿ was different in South Africa.
14. People have made gold coins and jewelry and later ＿＿＿＿＿＿ them into a liquid.

II. VOCABULARY (new context)

situations   seize   license   ancient
quantity   fortune   madness   cruel
throughout   rush   mine   distant
minerals   melts   decorations   last
sink

1. Iron and gold are both ＿＿＿＿＿＿.
2. Snow ＿＿＿＿＿＿ in the spring.
3. Do you have a driver's ＿＿＿＿＿＿?
4. A large amount of sap makes only a small ＿＿＿＿＿＿ of maple syrup.
5. If clothes are not good quality, they do not ＿＿＿＿＿＿ very long.
6. There is a large iron ＿＿＿＿＿＿ in northern Sweden.
7. People cry in different kinds of ＿＿＿＿＿＿.
8. People in large cities always seem to ＿＿＿＿＿＿ everywhere they go.
9. Sometimes people who are ＿＿＿＿＿＿ to their children have to go to prison.
10. It is traditional to put ＿＿＿＿＿＿ on a Christmas tree.
11. The ＿＿＿＿＿＿ Syrians discovered how to make glass.
12. New kinds of glass have been developed ＿＿＿＿＿＿ the twentieth century.
13. ＿＿＿＿＿＿ countries are only a few hours away by plane.
14. Queen Elizabeth owns a ＿＿＿＿＿＿ in jewelry.
15. Some European kings suffered from ＿＿＿＿＿＿.
16. ＿＿＿＿＿＿ every chance you have to speak English.
17. When the sun sets near the ocean, it seems to ＿＿＿＿＿＿ into the water.

III. VOCABULARY REVIEW

Match the words that are closest in meaning.

1. attempt
2. unite
3. marketing
4. invention
5. type
6. emperor
7. enlarge
8. hardships

a. discovery
b. king
c. buying and selling
d. suffering
e. try
f. obvious
g. kind
h. enforce
i. join
j. increase

IV. ORAL QUESTIONS

1. With what two minerals is gold most commonly found?
2. Give four reasons why early humans used gold.
*3. In what century did Europeans start getting gold from America?
4. Explain how to separate gold from sand.
5. Why did people rush to places that gold was discovered?
6. How was the South African gold rush different from the others?
7. Why is gold easy to work?
*8. Are most things made of gold essential? Could they be made from other materials?

V. COMPREHENSION: True/False/No Information (T/F/NI)

_____ 1. The Romans got their gold from Romania.
_____ 2. Both the Spanish and the Egyptians were cruel to their miners.
_____ 3. Gold probably came from great depths in the earth.
_____ 4. Gold is always the same color.
_____ 5. Early humans used gold because it was very easy to dig out of the ground.
_____ 6. The earliest gold mines were found in Syria.

_____ 7. It is easier to separate gold from sand than to dig it from the ground.

_____ 8. There is gold in sea water.

VI. MAIN IDEA

Read the three main ideas. Write the letter of each supporting detail under the correct main idea.

1. History of gold   2. Production methods   3. Uses of gold

a. Gold is reused.
b. The Spanish searched for gold in America.
c. South African mines use complicated machinery.
d. There was a gold rush in New Zealand.
e. It is easy to work gold into decorations.
f. Miners needed a license to mine on the Fraser River.
g. Use a pan to separate gold from sand.

WORD STUDY

I. PREPOSITIONS

Write the correct preposition in each blank.

1. Throughout history gold has been important _____ human society.
2. Men have killed _____ it.
3. People have gone _____ the distant corners _____ the earth.
4. The Spanish explored a new world _____ search _____ it.
5. A kind _____ madness seizes people when they think _____ gold.
6. Gold was _____ least partly _____ liquid form.
7. People could find gold _____ using tools _____ dig it _____ the ground.

8. It is very easy _____ separate gold _____ the sand _____ a
river.
9. Pour _____ some _____ the sand and water.
10. People heard stories _____ finding large pieces _____ gold lying
_____ the ground.

II. SUFFIXES: Words Ending in -ever

whatever = anything	whenever = any time
whoever = anyone	wherever = any place

Write the correct word in each sentence.

1. We can leave the party _____ you like.
2. I lent my book to someone in the class. Would _____ has
it please return it to me.
3. Order _____ you want for dinner.
4. You can go _____ you like on your vacation. Just take a
lot of money.

III. CONTEXT CLUES

Each underlined word has at least two meanings. Choose the meaning of
the word as it is used in this sentence.

1. There are so few dirty dishes that we can wash them in the <u>sink</u> instead
of using the dishwasher.
    a. a water container with pipes to let water in and out
    b. go down to the bottom of water
    c. a machine that washes dishes
    d. float
2. The final race will <u>last</u> one minute.
    a. continue for   c. run
    b. final   d. finish
3. Would you please <u>type</u> this letter for me? My handwriting is hard to read.
    a. mail   c. kind
    b. write using a machine d. read

4. The restaurant was <u>so far</u> from our apartment that it took forty minutes to drive there.
   a. very distant
   b. expensive
   c. no longer
   d. until now
5. Cities <u>throughout</u> the world are increasing in population.
   a. during
   b. knock over
   c. everywhere
   d. though

EARLY HUMANS

When did human life on Earth begin? How did humans survive the ice ages and other changes in climate? Why did humans survive when huge animals all died?

No one knows the answers to these questions exactly,

5 but archaeologists are attempting to find out. They study
the remains of villages where people lived thousands of
years ago. They <u>examine</u> the bones, <u>skulls</u>, tools, needles, (look at closely) (bones in the head)
and other things that they find in graves and <u>caves</u>. They
weigh and measure them, describe and photograph them.
10 They make tests to find out how old they are. Little by
little, as information is gathered throughout the world, we
are learning more about early humans.

   In 1964, Mary and Louis Leakey found a skull in East
Africa that was two million years old. They had worked
15 for years searching for, and studying the remains of, early
humans. In 1972 their son Richard found a skull a half
million years older. The skull is similar to a human skull,
and it appears that the person was like a modern human.
A few years later Richard Leakey found another skull

cave

20 that was 3 or 3.5 million years old. However, it is difficult
to decide whether it is from a human or an animal almost
like a human.

   It is hard to imagine how humans survived the difficult
life of those times. Humans have very little body hair to
25 keep the body warm. Animals are much better equipped
for cold weather. Human <u>skin</u> is very thin and can be hurt (covering of the body)
easily. Human teeth and <u>fingernails</u> are not strong like
animal teeth and toenails.

   However, humans have some advantages over ani-
30 mals. Humans learned to stand up. The fingers on the
hand are all separate. The <u>thumb</u> moves so the hand can
take hold of things and use tools.

thumb, fingernail

   Early humans learned to do things that animals cannot
do. They carved needles, <u>fishhooks</u>, and tools from bone
35 and ivory. Somehow someone discovered fire. They
learned to make a fire for heat and to cook their food. A
fire frightened away dangerous animals. They could also
use fire to harden the bone and wooden tools.

fishhook

   Early humans also decorated caves and rocks with pic-
40 tures. Even thousands of years ago, when life was very
difficult, art was essential to humans.

   Even more important, the human brain can remember.
Animals remember too, but not as much as humans. Humans can learn to do something, remember it, and use

tool

45 that <u>knowledge</u> to learn more. Then they can teach their   (noun for know)
children. In this way, human knowledge increases.

The first humans probably lived in small groups and
moved from place to place following animals. They were
hunters and gatherers.

50   How did they learn farming? Again, no one knows. It
probably took thousands of years for humans to change
from gatherers of wild plants to farmers. They still hunted
sometimes, but farming was more important. This was a
great change in human life—perhaps one of the most im-
55 portant changes in human history.

When people stayed in one place as farmers, they
were able to raise animals and build houses. Finally, the
group made rules to live by. This is when the group became a society. Thousands of years later people devel-
60 oped a system of writing. The oldest writing ever found
is 5,000 years old. Did people write before that? Perhaps
archaeologists will find some older writing in a cave
somewhere.

When people started to write, history began. It took
65 hundreds of thousands of years from the time humans
first began to make tools and build fires until they could
write. What changes will the next hundred thousand
years bring?

I. VOCABULARY

archaeologists	survive	exactly	skulls	graves
fingernails	knowledge	measure	raise	caves
advantages	fishhooks	brain	thumb	skin
examine				

1. How did humans _____ the ice ages?
2. No one knows the answers to these questions _____, but _____
   are attempting to find out.
3. They _____ the bones, _____, and tools they
   find in _____ and _____.
4. They weigh and _____ them.

5. Human _____ is very thin and can be hurt easily.
6. Human teeth and _____ are not strong.
7. However, humans have some _____ over animals.
8. The _____ moves so the hand can take hold of things.
9. Early humans carved needles, _____, and tools.
10. The human _____ can remember.
11. Humans can learn something and use that _____ to learn more.
12. They were able to _____ animals and build houses.

II. VOCABULARY (new context)

fingernails	fishhooks	measure	raise	thumb
advantages	knowledge	survived	brains	skin
archaeologists	exactly	grave	skull	caves
examined				

1. President Kennedy's _____ is near Washington, D.C.
2. Different races have different _____ color.
3. Parents want to give their children a good education and as many other _____ as possible.
4. People use _____ to catch fish.
5. People think with their _____.
6. Only ten people _____ the terrible bus accident.
7. The _____ and _____ are parts of the hand.
8. Students increase their _____ every day.
9. Please _____ the cupboards to see how much paint we need.
10. _____ study the remains of earlier humans and their societies.
11. The brain is inside the _____.
12. Farmers _____ crops and animals.
13. The doctor _____ the child to see why he was sick.
14. Some Indians in New Mexico lived in _____ in the side of mountains.

III. VOCABULARY REVIEW: Antonyms

Match the words that mean the opposite.

1. sink	a. unclear
2. smart	b. unintelligent
3. distant	c. divide
4. obvious	d. seize
5. ancient	e. float
6. unite	f. unlucky
7. cruel	g. near
8. fortunate	h. modern
	i. kind
	j. decision

IV. ORAL QUESTIONS

1. How do archaeologists learn about early humans?
2. How are animals better equipped than humans?
3. How are humans better equipped than animals?
4. Farmers lived a different kind of life from gatherers. Explain how it was different.
5. What makes a group of people a society?
6. Why do archaeologists examine graves?
*7. Why did early humans live in caves?
*8. Why was the development of a writing system so important?
9. Why was the discovery of fire so important?

V. COMPREHENSION

1. The oldest remains of someone that possibly was a person are _____ years old.
   a. two million
   b. 2½ million
   c. between 3 and 3½ million
   d. almost three million
2. Humans have _____.
   a. little body hair and strong fingernails
   b. thin skin and separated fingers
   c. strong fingernails and thick skin
   d. strong teeth and thumbs

3. Human knowledge increases because humans _____.
   a. can stand up
   b. discovered fire
   c. can remember
   d. carved fishhooks and tools
4. Gatherers _____.
   a. search for animals to kill
   b. search for plants to eat
   c. raise crops and animals
   d. make rules to live by
5. The oldest writing ever found is _____ years old.
   a. a half million
   b. 5,000
   c. hundreds of thousands
   d. 3,000
6. History began when people _____.
   a. started to write
   b. discovered fire
   c. started making rules to live by
   d. started to stand up
*7. Which one is probably NOT true?
   a. The discovery of fire was very important.
   b. Hunters and gatherers made large beautiful containers.
   c. Humans made tools because their hands and teeth were not strong enough without them.
   d. The thumb is an important advantage of humans over animals.

VI. MAIN IDEA: Supporting Details

Write the letter of each supporting detail under the correct main idea.

1) Human Qualities   2) Human Abilities   3) Human History

a. Humans can remember.
b. Humans carved stone tools.
c. Humans have a thumb.
d. Humans discovered fire.
e. Humans developed a writing system.
f. Humans have separated fingers.
g. Humans learned to farm.
h. Humans formed societies.
i. Humans made needles and fishhooks.

WORD STUDY

I. IRREGULAR VERBS

Learn these verb forms. Then put the correct form in each sentence.

Present	Past	Past Participle
1. hit	hit	hit
2. let	let	let
3. hang	hung	hung
4. fly	flew	flown
5. lead	led	led

1. Tom usually _____ at least two home runs in every baseball game.
2. Will you _____ me borrow your car?
3. Sarah usually _____ her coat in the closet.
4. Have you ever _____ in a small plane?
5. The judge _____ the two lawyers into his office for a short conference.

II. SUFFIXES: Noun + -ous = Adjective; Noun + -like = Adjective

A common ending is -ous, which means having or full of.

Spelling: Drop the final e.
Irregular: space—spacious

Another common heading is -like. There are no spelling changes for -like.

Add -ous to the words in the first column. Add -like to the words in the second column. Then write an adjective in each sentence.

Noun	Adjective	Noun	Adjective
joy	_____	life	_____
fame	_____	war	_____
danger	_____	child	_____
poison	_____		

1. It is _____ to eat some plants because they are _____.
2. Holidays are usually _____ times. No one has to work, there are family get-togethers, and people eat special food.
3. Muhammad Ali is a _____ boxer.
4. Eskimo carvings are _____. They look almost exactly the way real animals and people look.
5. In the 1930s Germany began to take _____ actions. Then in 1939 it attacked Poland and started a war.
6. It is sad that some people are born with very little intelligence. Even when they are grown-ups they are _____.

III. CONTEXT CLUES

1. When people started farming, it was a <u>revolutionary</u> change in human life.
   - a. very great
   - b. warlike
   - c. turning
   - d. crops
2. John says he is twenty-one years old, but he is <u>actually</u> only twenty.
   - a. active
   - b. soon
   - c. now
   - d. really
3. David asked his father to explain exactly how computers worked. His father <u>replied</u> that he did not know.
   - a. asked
   - b. answered
   - c. asked again
   - d. talked
4. Sometimes a doctor must send a <u>patient</u> to the hospital.
   - a. someone who doesn't mind waiting
   - b. nurse
   - c. someone getting medical help
   - d. medicine
5. The small boat developed a hole and sank fifty <u>fathoms</u> to the bottom of the ocean.
   - a. a measure of depth
   - b. a measure of length
   - c. a measure of width
   - d. a measure of height

COMPUTERS

Imagine that it is a few years in the future. You are studying English in a small college in a Midwestern state. The newspaper rarely has news about your country. In fact, it has very little foreign news, but this does not bother

5   you at all. You sit comfortably in your apartment, turn on
    your computer, and ask for the foreign news. The screen
    is <u>immediately</u> filled with news from all over the world.   (right away)

        The computer is a wonderful machine. It is the most
    important invention since the type of engine used in cars.
10 Today it has the greatest effect on science, industry, and
    business, but it is being used more and more in education
    and medicine. By the end of this century it will touch the
    lives of everyone, even people in distant villages. It is a
    revolutionary invention.
15   The oldest kind of computer is the <u>abacus</u>, used in
    China since the sixth century. In the seventeenth century
    an adding machine was invented, but the first large, mod-
    ern computer was built in 1937. A few years later a com-
    puter could do 5,000 additions per second. Now the
20 computations are so fast that they are measured in <u>nano</u>-   (one billionth)
    seconds.

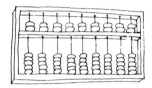

        Today most computers are stored-program computers;
    that is, they have a memory. They are getting smaller
    and smaller, and computing faster and faster. Even in a
25 large computer, the part that does the actual computing
    is about the size of the end of a finger.

        Computers can do all kinds of work. When someone
    buys something in a department store, information about
    the sale goes into a computer. During the night the com-
30 puter works on the information from all the sales that day.
    In the morning the manager has a report on everything
    that was sold and also on everything that must be re-
    ordered.

        All the information about the moon rocks is computer-
35 ized. A scientist can talk to the computer about the rocks,
    and the computer answers the questions. It is just like
    talking to another scientist.

        Another computer program has information about
    several kinds of diseases. A doctor can talk to the com-
40 puter and explain what is wrong with a patient. The com-
    puter explains what to do. If the doctor asks why, the
    computer goes through its stored information and explains
    exactly why. Again, it is just like talking to another human
    being.

45   Police stations have terminals connected to the National
Crime Information Center in Washington, D.C. A police
officer who stops a car can radio the station and learn
from the computer if the driver is a criminal or if the car is
stolen.

50   Telephone companies and banks use computers. In
some factories computerized <u>robots</u> do the work that
people used to do. For example, in an automobile factory,
when a different type of car comes along the line, the
robot changes the work that it does, just as a human

55 would do. Airline offices use computers. A person types
information about reservations on a terminal and gets an
immediate reply.

    When early humans began farming, it was a revolu-
tionary change in human life. It was hundreds of thou-

60 sands of years later that people developed a writing system. In less than fifty years people have developed computers that can do most of the things humans can do.
This could be a frightening development. Will we use
computers to control people and to make wars even

65 more terrible than they are now? Or will we use them to
improve the quality of life for all humanity? The students
of today will have to decide how to use the computers
of tomorrow.

I. VOCABULARY

terminals	manager	actual	robots
abacus	seconds	nanoseconds	in fact
bother	immediately	revolutionary	screen
connected	patient	reservations	reply

1. The newspaper has very little foreign news, but this does not _____ you at all.
2. The _____ is _____ filled with news from all over the world.
3. The computer is a _____ invention.
4. The oldest kind of computer is the _____.

5. Now computations are counted in _____.
6. The part that does the _____ computing is about the size of the end of a finger.
7. A doctor can explain what is wrong with a _____.
8. Police stations have _____ _____ to a computer in Washington, D.C.
9. In some factories computerized _____ do the work.
10. In airline offices a person types information about _____ on a terminal.
11. The person gets an immediate _____.

II. VOCABULARY (new context)

terminals	revolutionary	connected	screens
patients	actual	immediately	reservation
nanosecond	reply	bothers	abacus

1. The development of "new" plants may cause a _____ change in people's eating habits.
2. Noise _____ me when I am studying.
3. The new hospital can serve 100 _____ at a time.
4. Movies are shown on large _____.
5. We thought our new car would cost $8,000, but the _____ price was $8,600.
6. Leave the building _____ if the fire alarm rings.
7. Some computer _____ look like typewriters.
8. Did you make your plane _____?
9. The _____ to my letter came very quickly.
10. Pipes from maple trees are _____ to a storage tank.

III. VOCABULARY REVIEW

candle	flour	current	anyway
peanuts	scenery	boss	pails
warned	encouraged	bullet	icebergs

1. _____ contain oil and protein.
2. The _____ in the Rocky Mountains is beautiful.

3. Indians hung _____ on maple trees to catch the sap.
4. The Gulf Stream is a strong _____ in the Atlantic Ocean.
5. The police officer _____ the driver not to drive over the speed limit.
6. Mr. and Mrs. Walker _____ their daughter to enter the Miss World competition.
7. Paul's _____ asked him to work two hours overtime.
8. Amnesty International's _____ brings light and hope to prisoners.
9. _____ float north from Antarctica on ocean currents.
10. Bob didn't want to study on Sunday, but he had to do it _____.

IV. ORAL QUESTIONS

1. In what areas of modern life are computers used?
2. What kind of computers are most common today?
3. How are computers used in medicine?
4. How are they used in business?
5. How are they used in police work?
6. How could computers be dangerous to humanity?

V. COMPREHENSION

1. The computer is the most important invention since _____.
   a. farming
   b. writing
   c. glass
   d. a kind of engine
2. A stored-program computer has a _____.
   a. memory
   b. brain
   c. robot
   d. station
3. The part of a computer that _____ is the size of the end of a finger.
   a. prints the information
   b. stores the information
   c. does the computing
   d. thinks of the answer
4. Computer computations are measured in _____.
   a. seconds
   b. milliseconds
   c. microseconds
   d. nanoseconds

5. Computers will soon affect _____.
   a. people in large cities
   b. the population of developed countries
   c. all humanity
   d. the Western world

VI. MAIN IDEA

Choose the two main ideas.

_____ 1. Computers can do hundreds of kinds of work.
_____ 2. Computers are used in industry and business.
_____ 3. The computer is a wonderful invention that could be used for terrible purposes.

WORD STUDY

I. WORD FORMS

Verb	Noun	Adjective
1. die	death	dead
2. decorate	decoration	
3.	cruelty	cruel
4. describe	description	descriptive
5. breathe	breath	
6. compute	computer	
	computation	
7. reserve	reservation	
8. revolt	revolution	revolutionary
9. know	knowledge	
10. (dis)connect	connection	(dis)connected

Write the correct word form in each sentence.

1. President Kennedy is _____. He _____ in 1963.
2. In Canada people _____ a tree for Christmas.

3. Some governments are very _____ to people in prison.
4. Write a _____ of your home in your composition.
5. A beaver can hold its _____ for fifteen minutes.
6. The telephone company _____ the cost of your long distance calls every month.
7. Last night I _____ a hotel room for my trip to Washington.
8. Thirteen colonies _____ against England in 1776 and became the United States.
9. The amount of human _____ is increasing very fast.
10. I didn't pay my phone bill for three months and the telephone company _____ my phone.

II. WORD FORMS

This exercise is just for fun and it is difficult. See if you can figure out these words and put them in the correct sentences.

oversimplification   undereducated
discouraged   commercialized
unrecognizable   nonwarlike
programmer   multiplicity

1. Paula dressed in strange clothes and put a lot of makeup on her face for a party. She was completely _____.
2. The student says his country nationalized the foreign oil companies because they were stealing the oil. This is an _____ of the situation.
3. There is a _____ of problems in third world countries.
4. One problem is that most of the population is _____.
5. Carl is a computer _____ for a large company.
6. Christmas has become _____ in the United States.
7. Don't get _____ if you can't do this exercise.

III. CONTEXT CLUES

1. A diamond is a <u>gem</u>.
   a. glass
   b. jewel
   c. quartz
   d. necklace

2. The criminal tried to <u>flee</u> from the police officer.
   - a. run away
   - b. fly
   - c. a tiny animal
   - d. shout
3. Carl <u>sniffed</u> the air and knew something was burning.
   - a. smoked
   - b. listened to
   - c. smelled
   - d. tasted
4. The glass dish <u>toppled</u> off the shelf and broke.
   - a. opposite of bottom
   - b. fell
   - c. above
   - d. knocked
5. Millions of poor people live in <u>shacks</u> outside third world cities.
   - a. parks
   - b. small experimental farms
   - c. modern apartment buildings
   - d. small badly built homes

RULES FOR CHOOSING THE RIGHT WORD FORM

1. Every sentence must have a verb. Put a verb form in every sentence.

2. The subject of a sentence is a noun or pronoun.

   subject
   Eskimos live in northern Canada and Alaska.

3. The direct object of a verb is a noun or pronoun. It answers the question, "What?" It receives the action of the verb.

             direct object
   Families usually arranged marriages.
   What did families arrange? Marriages.
   Families arranged them.

4. The object of a preposition is a noun or a pronoun.

         noun
     prep object
   I talked to a stranger at the party.

       pronoun
    prep object
   I talked to her.

5. You can use the *-ing* form of a verb as a noun.

   subject
   Teaching is an interesting job.

      direct object
   John enjoys studying.

       object of prep
   You can learn more English by watching television.

6. Use a noun after an article (a, an, the). There may be an adjective before the noun.

      noun
   A bookstore sells books.

208

adj noun

A <u>large</u> <u>mall</u> has fifty to one hundred stores.

7. An adjective describes a noun or pronoun. An adjective is before the noun or after <u>be</u>.

   adj noun

   Her <u>new</u> <u>car</u> is in the parking lot.

   noun adj

   Her <u>car</u> is <u>red</u>.

pronoun adj

   <u>It</u> is <u>red</u>.

8. The past participle of a verb can be used as an adjective. The past participle of a regular verb is the <u>-ed</u> form.

   talk—talked

   Past participles of irregular verbs must be memorized.

   adj   noun

   Some languages have a <u>limited</u> vocabulary.

   noun   adj   adj

   Some languages are <u>spoken</u> but not <u>written</u>.

SPELLING RULES

1. Change the final *y* to *i* before:

-al	industry—industrial
-ly	day—daily
-ful	beauty—beautiful
-age	marry—marriage

2. Drop the final *y* before:

-ize	memory—memorize

3. When a word ends in silent *e*, drop the *e* before:

-ing	write—writing
-age	store—storage
-ous	fame—famous
-y	juice—juicy

4. Drop the *-le* on words ending in *-ble* before adding *-ly*.

                             probable—probably

5. The $1-1-1$ rule: When a word has one syllable with one vowel followed by one consonant, double the final consonant before adding:

-ing	swim—swimming
-en	fat—fatten
-er	big—bigger
-y	mud—muddy

PREPOSITIONS

to—shows movement

> She goes <u>to</u> class in the morning.
> John walked <u>to</u> a restaurant at noon.

at—shows location (place)

> She usually has dinner <u>at</u> home.

—shows time

> She usually has dinner <u>at</u> six o'clock.

in—inside something

> The cat is <u>in</u> the house.

—within limits of a space or time
> They have their vacation <u>in</u> April. (months)

He was born in 1962. (years)

People like to go swimming in summer. (seasons)

I'll meet you in ten minutes.

Note: in the morning   at noon
        in the afternoon   at night
        in the evening   at midnight
                                           at 7:00, 6:30, 4:23, and so on

on—over and touching something

The papers are on the desk.

—touching something

The clock is on the wall.

Note: on Monday (days)   on the radio
        on January 10 (dates)   on television
        in January (months)
        in spring (seasons)
        in 1945 (years)

of—belonging to things

the back of the room

the arm of the chair

BUT

John's arm (person)

—with numbers

one of the students

thousands of Southerners

—with definite and indefinite amounts

a lot of hamburgers

part of the house

half of the students

some of the country musicians

—shows a relationship between two nouns

the name of the city

a kind of store

an example of country music

by—near

The table is by the chair.

—along, through, over

They entered the building by the front door.

—not later than (time)

Please be here <u>by</u> 7:00 P.M. (at 7:00 or before 7:00 but not later than 7:00)

—as a result of

You can learn another language <u>by</u> studying. (Use the *-ing* form of the verb after a preposition *except to*.)

—travel

<u>by</u> plane	They went to Canada <u>by</u> plane.
<u>by</u> ship	
<u>by</u> bus	(Use <u>by</u> when it has only one word
<u>by</u> car	after it.)

BUT

<u>in</u> my car
<u>in</u> a car
<u>in</u> a friend's car
<u>on</u> my bicycle
<u>on</u> foot

BUT people usually say, "Walk."

"I come to class on foot" is correct, but people do not usually say this. They say, "I walk to class."

IRREGULAR VERBS

These are all of the irregular verbs that are in the lessons.

Present	Past	Past Participle	Common Noun Forms
bear	bore	born	birth
become	became	become	
begin	began	begun	beginning
blow	blew	blown	
break	broke	broken	break
bring	brought	brought	
build	built	built	building
buy	bought	bought	
catch	caught	caught	catch
choose	chose	chosen	choice
come	came	come	
dig	dug	dug	
do/does	did	done	
drink	drank	drunk	drink
drive	drove	driven	
eat	ate	eaten	
fall	fell	fallen	fall
feel	felt	felt	feeling
fight	fought	fought	fight
find	found	found	
forget	forgot	forgotten	
fly	flew	flown	flight
get	got	got	
give	gave	given	gift
go/goes	went	gone	
grow	grew	grown	growth
hang	hung	hung	
have/has	had	had	
hear	heard	heard	
hide	hid	hidden	
hold	held	held	

Present	Past	Past Participle	Common Noun Forms
keep	kept	kept	
know	knew	known	knowledge
lead	led	led	
leave	left	left	
lie	lay	lain	
lose	lost	lost	loss
make	made	made	
mean	meant	meant	meaning
meet	met	met	meeting
ring	rang	rung	
rise	rose	risen	
say	said	said	
see	saw	seen	sight
sell	sold	sold	sale
send	sent	sent	
shake	shook	shook	
shine	shone	shone	shine
shoot	shot	shot	shot
sing	sang	sung	song
sink	sank	sunk	
sit	sat	sat	
speak	spoke	spoken	speech
spend	spent	spent	
stand	stood	stood	
steal	stole	stolen	
swim	swam	swum	swimming
take	took	taken	
teach	taught	taught	teaching
tell	told	told	
think	thought	thought	thought
understand	understood	understood	understanding
wear	wore	worn	
win	won	won	
write	wrote	written	writing

VOCABULARY

O

obsidian, **178**
obviously, **155**
ocean, **55**
order, **63**
ordinary, **30**
organization, **114**
overcrowded, **74**
ownership, **157**

P

pail, **164**
pain, **91**
parking lot, **14**
patient (n), **201**
peanut, **108**
penguin, **140**
per, **99**
percent, **6**
perfume, **91**
persuade, **123**
pineapple, **57**
pipe, **164**
place (v), **148**
poison, **149**
polite, **115**
pond, **132**
population, **65**
pour, **164**
prepare, **141**
pressure, **115**
prevent, **73**
print, **115**
prize, **115**
produce, **38**
program, **30**
protein, **107**
protect, **123**
provide, **74**
purpose, **155**

Q

quality, **6**
quantity, **185**
quartz, **178**

R

rabbit, **82**
race, **57**
raise, **194**
realize, **38**
related, **63**
relative (n), **38**
religion, **114**
remains, **124**
remarry, **38**
repair, **131**
reply, **202**
reservation, **202**
residential, **14**
revolutionary, **201**
rice, **107**
robot, **202**
roll, **47**
rudely, **148**
rush, **185**

S

sap, **164**
scenery, **123**
screen, **201**
seal, **47**
search, **56**
seed, **99**
seize, **185**
separate, **38**
serious, **57**

serve, **6**
service, **6**
shake (n), **6**
shampoo, **91**
sharp, **132**
sheep, **82**
sheet, **178**
shelf, **171**
similar, **73**
simple, **29**
sink (v), **185**
situation, **186**
skin, **193**
skull, **193**
smart, **29**
smooth, **47**
so (much), **29**
so (that), **38**
so far, **115**
social, **37**
society, **37**
soil, **123**
solution, **107**
solve, **107**
sorrow, **148**
soybean, **107**
special, **47**
speech, **63**
spout, **164**
spread, **132**
spring (water), **123**
steer, **132**
still (yet), **6**
storage, **164**
stream, **131**
stretch, **46**
studio, **30**
suffer, **149**
suggest, **114**
suitable, **107**
supplies, **22**
survive, **192**
syrup, **164**
system, **63**

T

tank, **164**
tax, **22**
tear (crying), **148**
temperature, **171**
teosinte, **108**
terminal, **202**
terrible, **148**
though, **124**
throughout, **184**
thumb, **193**
tiny, **140**
tool, **178**
topsoil, **123**
towel, **14**
toy, **14**

traditional, **30**
trap, **133**
trial, **115**
type (kind), **178**

U

unfortunately, **73**
unite, **157**
use up, **99**

V

value, **141**
violence, **114**
volcano, **178**

W

warn, **132**
waterfall, **123**
whale, **47**
wheat, **107**
whether, **108**
wildlife, **124**
wing, **107**
winged bean, **107**
worth, **30**

Y

yet (but), **82**

INDEX OF PREFIXES
AND SUFFIXES